GATEWAY *to* GRACE

Connecting the **Ten Commandments** to Everyday Life

CARRIE SANCHEZ

Foreword by Fr. Zachary Burns, T.O.R.

Visit the author's website at www.carriesanchez.net

Editor: Katelin Cummins
Graphic Designer: Rosemary Strohm
Book Cover by Kira Sanchez—*Transfiguration* by Raphael
First edition 2026

ISBN: 979-8-9941469-0-3 (paperback)
ISBN: 979-8-9941469-1-0 (ebook)

CONTENTS

Foreword

During my seminary years, one of my most oft-watched films was Carlo Carlei's three-and-a-half hour epic, *Padre Pio: Miracle Man.* I remember being especially captivated by the rawness of the scenes which took place within the confessional. The soul-searing inquisitiveness of the future Saint as he deftly poked and prodded at the hearts of tearful penitents like a divine surgeon inspired me greatly.

At the start of my own priestly ministry, I encountered a perplexing dilemma. St. Paul–one of the greatest saints in the history of the Church–insisted that he was the most wretched of all sinners. Yet well-intentioned penitents would come to the confessional and nervously struggle to remember more than one or two sins committed over a multi-year period. It didn't add up. In my mind, there were two possibilities: either people *weren't sinning* or they didn't fully understand that they were sinners. I suspected the latter, but I struggled to know how to broach the topic. How does one even begin?

Enter our author, Carrie Sanchez. Although there are many talented individuals at our parish, I've long seen Carrie as someone with a heightened prophetic sensibility–a woman with a finger on the spiritual pulse of the laity and clergy, alike. For this reason, we would often meet informally in my office to discuss all manner of things related to evangelization.

Gateway to Grace was inspired by Carrie's role facilitating our parish's *Catechism in a Year* weekly discussion group when our pastor was reassigned mid-year. Even though I was slated to take over, in my own personal prayer, I felt the Lord telling me that although the program was doing just fine in its current format, it was time for a true change of pace.

Theologically-inclined pastor-led lectures would give way to boots-on-the-ground discussion. Teaching would give way to mentorship. Who better to help the laity navigate their way through the complex web of Catholic morality than one of their own: a married mother of four confronting, in real time, so many of the demanding moral benchmarks upheld by the Church.

Carrie's love and passion for God and her fellow parishioners was palpable.

The fruit was immediate, especially in the place I most hoped to find it: the confessional. As more and more parishioners were encountering the life-giving moral teachings of the Catholic Church in a relevant, conversational, and down-to-earth way from someone they saw first and foremost as a fellow parishioner, the quality (and quantity) of the confessions I heard seemed to rise dramatically.

While at one time it seemed that many confessing their sins really didn't even know if they were, in fact, sinners at all, they now opened their confessions with lines like, "Father! I had no idea this thing I was doing throughout my whole marriage was a sin! I can't believe I never heard about this. Why did nobody ever teach it to me?!"

Two bold questions that take courage to ask are: *Do I realize how great a sinner I really am? Do I realize how I am in dire need of God's mercy?*

We live in a culture where such inquiry is taboo. We don't talk about sin, faults, and failures. In his letter to the Ephesians, St. Paul exhorts us to "say only the good things that men need to hear–things that will truly help them." Unfortunately we've collectively taken this to mean that to affirm someone is "good" and to challenge someone is "bad." Therefore, to help someone see that they are a sinner in need of God's mercy, and to aid them in understanding the intricacies of the moral life to which God calls each of us as an alternative to sin, is "off-limits."

My experience, though, is that Christian morality sets us free. The pursuit of perfection brings us joy. To live within God's parameters gives us a sense of purpose and direction. Thus, to understand that we are all sinners being called to a clear standard of moral conduct is not oppressive, but liberating. Just because it may be difficult for us to soberly confront our sin, it doesn't mean that we shouldn't be shown the ways in which we are sinners. It doesn't mean that our moral blind spots should be safeguarded or ignored. Moral clarity is Christian charity. It fits well within the category of "good things that men need to hear."

I can assure you that what I was now encountering in the confessional was anything but oppressive guilt; it was freedom. Because to know Catholic morality is not just to know rules. It's not just to know what we can and cannot do. To know Catholic morality is to know the mind and heart of God. Nothing He commands us to do through His words in scripture or teaches through His Holy Church is arbitrary. None of it is for our suffering or enslavement.

God's law gives us life. It helps us to understand our purpose and our destiny. It aids us in understanding the natural order of the created world around us and our place in that order. The freest person is the one who knows God's will, understands how he has fallen short of it, and through the help of God's mercy and grace, amends his life so that he may live in accordance with it.

I hope that the rawness and realness of Carrie's words resonate with you. I pray you will experience the freedom that comes from knowing the Father's heart. And I believe *Gateway to Grace* will unleash the floodgates of grace into your life.

—Fr. Zachary Burns, T.O.R.

Preface

I stepped out into the darkness, the cold concrete beneath my feet. The black of night ripped open with a flash of lightning. The thunder clapped, not in one loud expected bang, but as if the heavens watched and murmured their thoughts, muffled so I couldn't hear distinctly. One slow thunder echoed on as another lightning flashed. Slowly the sky sprinkled its weighty words encouraging me to string them together to write the story that wanted to be written.

If you think, "what an odd way to begin a book about the Commandments," then we will be great friends!

My favorite sentence in the entire *Catechism of the Catholic Church* is the very first one. "God, infinitely perfect and blessed in himself, in a plan of sheer goodness freely created man to make him share in his own blessed life."[1] This incredible truth bears repeating—God created us to share in his own blessed life.

My life is like one of my favorite pastimes—riding a rollercoaster of excitement, unknowns, twists, and turns. Our lives continually unfold as an adventure filled story that is penned every day. Miracles are not a thing of the past. No, God continues to work miracles even now. The very proof is right here in this book. You see, I was totally a *CliffsNotes* English student in high school and college. Not in a million years would I ever call myself a writer.

---

1 https://www.vatican.va/archive/ENG0015/__P2.HTM

Recently I was fortunate to be on a call with one of my favorite authors, Ralph Martin. When he was asked about being a writer, his response struck a chord in my heart. He said, "I don't really consider myself a writer. Sometimes the Lord inspires me to put into writing something that is particularly useful, or important, or needed right now, in my opinion, for the Church. I'm not a writer. From time to time the Lord lets me know that something He's giving me to see, something I've been talking about needs to be put into writing so that more people can benefit from it."[2]

Similarly, this book is a collection of stories and conversations I've had with the Lord over many years. At God's inspiration, they have now made it onto paper with the express purpose to share how learning, understanding, and living the Commandments has radically changed me and my life. I have come to understand that the Commandments stand as the gateway to grace. God perpetually pours out His grace upon all of His people. We each have a choice to either shield or saturate ourselves from or in His grace. As we stand in this torrential downpour of grace we have a choice. We either open up a huge umbrella to shield us from life-giving water, or widely outstretch our arms to capture every drop that falls from the sky.

As we journey through this book together, it is my hope that you will see how when we actively choose to know, and then subsequently live the Commandments, it unleashes the floodgates of grace into our lives. No longer do the Commandments appear as a list of rules, but become for us the very portal to live a supernatural life, infused with the spirit, and a heart that overflows with love. We live in times of division and strife, and it's easy to be anxious about so many concerns. However, by delving into the Commandments, we can navigate these often scary waters with the peace and confidence that comes with God's light as our guide along the way.

2 https://www.writethesewords.com/products/praisewriters-insider-interviews-library/categories/2154642535/posts/2182225385

As I glance in the rearview mirror of my own life, I see how God embraced me as I was. Every time I handed Him the oars, little by little He led me to greater understanding and love. I was reared in a Catholic home, but as many in my generation experienced, for a variety of reasons, my faith seemed to remain surface level. When I look back at my childhood, a particular memory of my dad's response to help me with homework stands out.

I was a very social child and yet also desired academic success. Every time I needed help with homework, a war raged within me between wanting a quick answer—so I could go out with friends—and choosing to slow down to learn the material. I always hoped my dad would just give me the quick answer. Inevitably however, each request of homework help was met with a deep inhale followed by the words, "let's open up your textbook, read the explanation, and walk through the logic together."

My dad's desire and ability to explain the "why" was extremely formative to the way I view and interact with the world now: an adult charged to discover and understand my faith to effectively pass it onto future generations. I can see how God infused me with desire and trained me to understand the "why" through those very mundane and secular early experiences with my dad.

Fast forward to when Ascension Press's *"Catechism in a Year"* podcast launched. I experienced that same excitement to delve into the "whys" of our Catholic faith. A desire burned deep within to help gather our parishioners at my home parish to collectively listen to the podcast and heed Fr. Mike Schmitz's call to listen to the podcast with our hearts and not just our heads; not to be informational only, but to allow God's word and Church teaching to truly be transformational in our lives.

In 2023, our parish filled the fellowship hall with nearly 120 people every week to journey with our pastor as we listened to Fr. Mike Schmitz unpack the treasures of the *Catechism* in his *"Catechism in a Year"* podcast. The most unexpected turn occurred when our Pastor was reassigned mid-year, at the conclusion of the second Pillar of the *Catechism*. The daunting task to facilitate our parish-wide weekly meetings to discuss *"Catechism in a Year"* (CIY) fell to me.

Pillar 3 of the *Catechism* is all about the moral life: in other words, sin. I'm in awe of God's timing of transition to enlist a lay person to facilitate these discussions. While every person, religious and lay alike, has to battle against sin, our families, as the domestic church, are under enormous attack. It was such a gift to not only journey with these faith-filled parishioners, but what the Lord worked on in my own heart and faith journey was nothing less than astounding.

Facilitating CIY felt like a great party to me; a joyous exploration of the Lord's loving instruction with friends who were eager to really allow these teachings to penetrate our hearts and minds. I witnessed the Holy Spirit tenderize and convert hearts in powerful ways during our time together. Very wise and faithful Catholics shared how they viewed Church teachings so differently as a result of our discussions.

They were inspired and invigorated to change the way they interacted with family and friends to breathe new life into their relationships with the wind of the Holy Spirit at their back. In the final week of facilitating the *"Catechism in a Year"* podcast discussion group, I also felt the tug of the Lord to a new and exciting adventure. This book is that awesome adventure.

In this book, together we will explore God's love for us, as revealed through the Ten Commandments and as highlighted in Pillar 3 of the *Catechism*. I highly encourage and recommend you read the *Catechism* in its entirety as part of your own journey to deepen your faith life. I also invite you to journey through Ascension Press' *"Catechism in a Year"* podcast, as it is so rich and accessible.

Through the study of Scripture, the *Catechism*, and sharing stories of my own life, and those of friends that have given their permission for me to share, I hope you can see yourself in my story, our story, Christ's story.

God is present in every one of our stories, whether we knew it or not at the time. Our stories, the good and the difficult alike, aren't meant to be hidden, but rather shared to light the way as a beacon for each other. I invite you to read these chapters with an open heart and mind. It may challenge you; it certainly challenged me, and still does. Together we can ask God to pour the Holy Spirit and His grace into our hearts to heal our very real hurts, brokenness, and places of sin, to empower us to embrace the abundant life He has promised.

I am no theologian. Rather, I resemble the young boy who eagerly offers the five barley loaves and two fish. I offer what little I have to the Lord to work His miracles. I am simply His little one who loves Him and wants to walk in His ways. I have dared to open my heart in vulnerability to God.

This book is one woman's ongoing journey to learn, stumble, and get up again and again. Our simple stories can, in Christ's loving hands, offer each other solidarity, tears, laughter, inspiration, and hope. May you, through my simple offering, come to know our good, good Father. The Father who loves you and always calls you to Himself, in new and fresh ways to His glory and grace.

How to Use This Book

This book offers help for you to grow in your ability to identify and repent of sin by walking alongside you through the Ten Commandments as presented in the third pillar of the *Catechism*. If you will read the chapters that follow with an open heart and mind, you may discover that the Commandments come alive in new ways that perhaps you hadn't previously considered. I will invite you to read selections from the *Catechism* in each chapter. Then I will expound and offer a real-life example or story to provide context and a deeper dive into the topic.

Throughout each chapter I will direct you to read parts directly from the *Catechism*. I abbreviate *Catechism of the Catholic Church* as CCC. For example, the instruction "read CCC 1700" indicates you are asked to read paragraph 1700 from the *Catechism*.

You can access the *Catechism* online or use a print copy. I utilized the printed *Catechism of the Catholic Church, Ascension Edition*. There are several online editions including https://www.usccb.org/sites/default/files/flipbooks/catechism/. It is also possible to utilize your browser's search feature to find the referenced paragraph. For example, type "CCC 1700" in your search bar and it will provide various online options of the *Catechism* for you to read and reference.

Each chapter concludes with some thought provoking questions. You can spend time in prayer with them, journal on your own, or utilize the companion Reconciliation journal offered when you purchased this book. Finally, at the conclusion of each chapter I created an Examination of Conscience that you can use in Confession and come back to reference when needed.

One final note before diving in. The supplemental Reconciliation journal companion was specifically created to give you a concrete place to encounter the Lord. It contains both the reflection questions and the Examination of Conscience found at the end of each chapter. It is a place where you have the freedom to dialogue with the Lord. I hope it becomes for you a sacred space where the Lord shows you where you've been, where you are going, and how much He delights and loves you.

Jesus famously said, "Repent and believe in the Gospel" (Mark 1:15). You will notice I use the terms Confession and Sacrament of Reconciliation interchangeably throughout the book. Take a moment to read the *Catechism's* terms for the official title, The Sacrament of Penance and Reconciliation found in CCC 1422-1424. There are five names used for this sacrament: sacrament of conversion, sacrament of Penance, sacrament of confession, sacrament of forgiveness, and sacrament of Reconciliation. Each term beautifully describes the profound and expansive dimensions of this wonderful gift. Every time we obey the Lord's command to "Repent and believe in the Gospel," we open the floodgates of grace.

INTRODUCTION

Am I *Really* a Sinner?

The question both I and others have frequently asked is, "What is this all for?" In a homily, one of my parish priests, Fr. Zachary Burns, T.O.R., said the question he gets asked the most is, "How do I know if I am hearing the voice of God?" He said it is usually asked with a sheepish embarrassment, and he compassionately responds, "If you aren't asking this question, why not? It is a good question and it is good that you are asking it." I think these two questions go hand in hand. "What is this all for and how do I know if I am hearing the voice of God?"

God wants us to hear Him. God constantly pursues us and our hearts to invite us into a relationship with Him. In many ways, it's remarkably simple. But do not be deceived; while it may be simple, it is far from easy! In fact, to seek, grow, maintain and intensify this relationship with the Lord is the veritable answer to the question, "What is this all for?" It is also absolutely the most difficult yet fulfilling endeavor one can pursue. "Seek first the kingdom [of God] and His righteousness, and all these things will be given you besides" (Matthew 6:33).

There are so many wonderful ideas to explore, but this book dives into one of the greatest obstacles to hear the voice of God: sin. This is not a fun or feel-good topic at all, but a must for those who truly and humbly seek to live life abundantly as He has promised us in

John 10:10, "A thief comes only to steal and slaughter and destroy; I came so that they might have life and have it more abundantly."

Psalm 118:19-21 states, "Open the gates of righteousness; I will enter and thank the Lord. This is the Lord's own gate, through it the righteous enter. I thank you for you answered me; you have been my savior."

John 1:16 states, "From his fullness we have all received, grace upon grace, because while the law was given through Moses, grace and truth came through Jesus Christ." This verse emphasizes that through Jesus, believers receive not just one instance of grace, but a constant, continuous, and abundant flow of God's favor and blessings, one after another.

The Commandments stand as the gateway to grace. Through our Baptism we are given the capacity to be saturated in God's grace. God's abundant love of our personal freedom and dignity has also given us free will to accept or reject His grace. When we understand and submit ourselves in obedience to the Commandments, we fling the gates wide open to penetrate our heart and our lives with His divine grace.

As we begin our journey together it is imperative to open your *Catechism* and read paragraphs 1987-1995. This section defines and explains grace, justification, and righteousness. The best summary of justification I have heard is, "salvation comes through discipleship." Grace is infused into us giving us supernatural power to live supernatural lives.[3] CCC 1993 states, "Justification establishes the cooperation between God's grace and man's freedom."

Jesus has paid the ultimate price. Through His life, death, and resurrection, He has purchased for us the reward of eternal salvation. He has won victory over sin and death. He offers and invites us to accept this incredible saving gift through the Sacrament of Baptism. As adopted sons and daughters we are given every grace to

3 Whitehead, Jason. 2025. St. Junipero Serra Institute. New Testament Survey Course. Session Five.

participate in His Divine Life, overcoming sin and darkness in our lives. 2 Timothy 1:7 emphatically reminds us, "For God did not give us a spirit of cowardice but rather of power and love and self-control."

This is no ordinary gift.

Take a moment to recall a childhood gift you looked forward to receiving with much anticipation. I remember my son's face beaming with excitement when he unwrapped his first remote-controlled car. He spent hours building ramps, obstacle courses, and pushed that car to its limits! Until one day, like the other gifts that had come before, it was set aside.

Jesus's grace is not a gift that we will ever outgrow. Just like His word—His grace is living and active! We are invited to accept and perpetually use His gift in our daily lives. When we remain docile to His Spirit, our lives embody a life of adventure!

Everyday the Lord invites us to recognize, accept, receive, and use His gift of grace. He has won victory—it is our choice to accept His grace and timely help to participate in His saving work. Every day is filled with choices to cooperate with His grace.

God gives us the blueprint of what this is all for and how to achieve the goal of eternal life with Him in Heaven. God is a gracious God, never outdone in generosity. Not only does He provide the blueprint for eternal life, but He also provides the blueprint of how to participate in the divine life in our everyday lives in the here and now. Every day God offers us His grace to bring His kingdom on earth, today—in your life and in mine.

If this excites you, we must spend time and attention in consideration of the ways we stunt our growth. Simply put—sin stunts our growth. When we sin, it is simultaneously like opening an umbrella in a rainstorm and stuffing earplugs in our ears—all of a sudden we block the downpour of grace from on high and we can no longer hear God's voice clearly.

Here is a common dynamic that plays out in our daily lives: God perpetually pours His grace upon us. We block it with our sin.

We are offered the opportunity to change this dynamic.

Many of us have a vague notion of what sin is and we have all too often been satisfied with thinking that is good enough. The shocking reality of this problem is that it opens the door to confusion and attack. Satan desires to intertwine our sin with our identity. This debilitates us. By keeping us intellectually in the dark about sin, Satan can play on our emotions, fears, and insecurities. He uses shame to affix our identity to our sin. If we identify with our sin so profoundly, we forget the victory that Jesus accomplished over our sin.

Conversely, when we understand what sin is—something separate and distinct, with its own identity—that brings clarity. Sin is a choice; not an identity. Knowing, accepting, and taking accountability for our choice to sin inherently separates our identity from the sin's identity. We can see ourselves separate and distinct from sin. This distinction gives us power over the enemy's lies and deceptions.

This book sails alongside you to inform your intellect. When you choose to read this book you embark upon an adventure that will unlock the power of your Baptism and faith. Your commitment to intellectually understand what the Ten Commandments reveal to us about sin is the first and a major step to properly dispose yourself to invite God's grace to transform your heart in repentance and love. It allows you to overcome sin not through your own power, but from a place of victory that Jesus has already won.

I promise, if you stay with me through this book, the Lord will bless you abundantly. This gift will transcend the ways of the world. You will know how to live in a state of grace that unleashes active participation in the Divine Life. You will hear God's voice more clearly and He will actively guide your steps. God will fill you with a deep abiding love and peace that comes from knowing you are loved, forgiven, and delighted in with every moment and effort you choose to give Him. This is awesome!

The Scripture read at daily Mass on the Feast of the Holy Innocents struck me like lightning. I immediately turned to my daughter and said, "This is the centerpiece of the book I sense the Lord is inviting me to write." It's important to read these words as though you are hearing them for the first time and simultaneously as though you have heard them one thousand times.

I encourage you to pray the following small prayer and then read the Scripture passage slowly and out loud.

> *Come, Holy Spirit. Help me hear and understand your Word in a deeper and new way than I have before. Open my heart and mind to allow your words to saturate my heart and mind and see you with new eyes. I ask this in Jesus' name. Amen.*

1 John 1:5-2:2 says,

> Beloved: This is the message that we have heard from Jesus Christ and proclaim to you: God is light, and in Him there is no darkness at all. If we say, "We have fellowship with Him, "while we continue to walk in darkness, we lie and do not act in truth. But if we walk in the light as He is in the light, then we have fellowship with one another, and the Blood of his Son Jesus cleanses us from all sin. If we say, "We are without sin," we deceive ourselves, and the truth is not in us. If we acknowledge our sins, He is faithful and just and will forgive our sins and cleanse us from every wrongdoing. If we say, "We have not sinned," we make Him a liar, and His word is not in us.
>
> My children, I am writing this to you so that you may not commit sin. But if anyone does sin, we have an Advocate with the Father, Jesus Christ the righteous one. He is expiation for our sins, and not for our sins only but for those of the whole world.

This Scripture passage both convicts me and consoles me. I hear the Lord's invitation to allow His words to wash over me, as well as penetrate my heart and mind. I don't know about you, but I find it so easy to justify my own sins, and in fact, falsely believe that some days I may not even sin at all.

Some days I may be so consumed in my own thoughts and ideas of what "needs" to get done, that I fail to recognize the harshness in my voice to my husband or children. Perhaps work drama is at an all time high and instead of praying for the good of everyone involved, I allow myself to be sucked into gossip. There are so many opportunities and traps that befall us every day. As 1 Peter 5:8 reminds us, "Be sober and vigilant. Your opponent the devil is prowling around like a roaring lion looking for [someone] to devour." That someone is me; that someone is you.

In those moments especially, I am so thankful that over time I have seen what is true in the light so I don't deceive myself in the darkness. It's in those moments that I am thankful that God has given me the grace to take up the cross of disciplined prayer, repentance, and humility. For without those graces, I would be swept along a roaring river of darkness, despair, and hopelessness that accompany sin.

Just as my dad would explain the "why" behind math problems, we are called to intentionally understand firstly, what the Commandments are, and secondly, why God has commanded them. *Catechism* paragraphs 142-144 help us to understand that faith is an assent of the intellect. We have heard some people say they have blind faith. I understand and appreciate that sentiment. I am naturally an obedient person and may agree to believe something that sounds reasonable. However, to have true faith, the Lord invites us to intellectually, logically, and academically understand His Commandments—and why he's given them to us. When we intellectually assent to the truth, we can leverage that intellect to reign and govern our passions and will. That allows us to choose the ultimate good He has shown us.

After we have gone through this process to inform ourselves about the "why" God has given us the Commandments, our gracious God, through his Church, also offers us the "how" to live them out.

Read CCC 2340. It articulates the "how" we are to "fight the good fight" in the battle against sin. It gives us extremely helpful words of advice and wisdom. If we truly want to love God, ourselves, and our neighbor, we need to put in the effort. We have to develop self-knowledge. We must begin with the simple act of noticing and taking inventory of our various triggers or reactions to certain people, words, or situations. We continue to mature to the deeper self-knowledge when we discover the root causes of those reactions.

We are served well to practice ascesis, which is self discipline. That can be any and everything from moderation of food and drink, fasting from media, food, or other pleasures, or delayed gratification in a variety of areas. We have to not only be obedient to God's Commandments, but go through the effort and time of first learning what they even are and how they apply to our lives (which hopefully you can glean from this book!)

We have to do the work to learn what the moral virtues are and how we can practice them. Finally, we have to put in the time and fidelity to pray to receive every ounce of grace that the Lord offers us in these endeavors. I echo the sentiment to be ruthless in our environment of sin. An unknown priest once said, *"Determined prayer and determined sin cannot co-exist; one will kill the other."* Are you willing to fully commit daily, even moment by moment, and invoke the Holy Spirit to come to your assistance and make haste to help you? If you add your dedicated efforts to the power of the Holy Spirit, amazing transformations happen.

These graces allow me to recognize my sinfulness. Instead of being devoured by my sins, I can acknowledge them, repent of them, and follow Him who rescues me from them. Jesus has certainly saved us from our sins—but that also requires us to acknowledge that we are in need of a Savior. If we were righteous in every way, we would not need Him.

That is not the case for me, and I hope that through God's grace you might come to the same conclusion about yourself. We do need a Savior and we do need Him as an Advocate to show us the way.

John 14:26 reminds us that "The Advocate, the Holy Spirit that the Father will send in my name—He will teach you everything and remind you of all that [I] told you." God wants to restore us. God wants to heal us. His love is fruitful and strong. His Ten Commandments are given to us as a gift to recognize not only the goal, but actually how to achieve this vision of love.

When we abide by the Commandments, we help to repair this broken world and manifest the kingdom of heaven here on earth. I don't know about you, but that excites me! That gives me a purpose to hope for and to work towards. I have a loving Father who has provided all the means for love; I just have to respond by being receptive to learn and grow with Him.

God is love. When I strip all the distractions away, love is fundamentally what I seek. It is what we long for. I think many of us in our youth envision a life of love. We will find a man or a woman with whom we can share our love and create a family—where children are like olive plants[4], filled with joy, happiness, and gratitude. And then we enter into the messy reality of this perfect vision.

Where does it go wrong? Sin. My sin, your sin, our sins, their sins, sins of our parents, sins of our friends, sins of strangers—all these attack this vision of love. But God has given us a remedy.

JESUS.

Jesus is the good news. Jesus established the Church to help guide us along the way in conjunction with the Holy Spirit to come and have life abundantly! When you strive to identify your sins, confess, and repent, you will experience the unleashing of grace into your life. You will find and experience the rich, abundant life and relationship with God that you desire!

Ready to dive in? Grab your *Catechism of the Catholic Church* and let's begin!

---

4 https://bible.usccb.org/bible/psalms/128

Framework to Understand the Commandments

To understand the Commandments, we first need to understand sin. The *Catechism* clearly defines sin in paragraphs 1849 and 1850:

> **1849** Sin is an offense against reason, truth, and right conscience; it is failure in genuine love for God and neighbor caused by a perverse attachment to certain goods. It wounds the nature of man and injures human solidarity. It has been defined as "an utterance, a deed, or a desire contrary to the eternal law."
>
> **1850** Sin is an offense against God: "Against you, you alone, have I sinned, and done that which is evil in your sight."Sin sets itself against God's love for us and turns our hearts away from it. Like the first sin, it is disobedience, a revolt against God through the will to become "like gods," knowing and determining good and evil. Sin is thus "love of oneself even to contempt of God." In this proud self-exaltation, sin is diametrically opposed to the obedience of Jesus, which achieves our salvation.

I appreciated Fr. Mike Schmitz's assertion, *"Sin is choosing ourselves over God and others."*[5] This is a heavy statement, but true.

Living in sin, great and small, is akin to living a mediocre life, worry to worry, problem to problem. Most sin usually stems from good, God-given desires that we, through a variety of reasons and means, have

5 https://www.youtube.com/watch?v=2Mr4na4vOGc

distorted. The *Catechism* goes into extensive lengths to explain The Fall and Original Sin in paragraphs 385-421. The first half of CCC 400 summarizes this result of sin powerfully:

> **400** The harmony in which they had found themselves, thanks to original justice, is now destroyed: the control of the soul's spiritual faculties over the body is shattered; the union of man and woman becomes subject to tensions, their relations henceforth marked by lust and domination. Harmony with creation is broken: visible creation has become alien and hostile to man.

In other words, the result of our sins is a dulled conscience and broken and hurt relationships, both with each other and creation itself. God wants us to have good and restored relationships.

When we look at each Commandment and the "why" behind them, we can see that they are not there to limit or confine us. Rather, God established the Commandments to give us the vision and tools to fully flourish personally and in our relationships. To know and obey the Commandments empowers us to truly embrace and become the absolutely unique and wonderfully made person God lovingly crafted us to be from the beginning of time and help others do the same.

Let those words you just read linger in your mind. Take a moment to envision a time or situation that elicits pure peace and joy. If you are like me, I immediately think of the big moments: marriage, the birth of a child etc., but when I'm honest, even those powerful moments seem to fade quickly.

When I reflect upon what leaves me with lasting peace and joy, it isn't moments but rather, relationships. This deep sense of peace and joy most often involves some kind of encounter within a relationship transparently and authentically 'seeing another' and 'being seen.' Delight is at the center of truly being seen—delight in another and feeling their genuine delight in me. I am grateful that I have experienced it in several relationships in my life.

On the flip side, I can tell you the loneliest times I have experienced are when I have desired to share my heart with someone and they didn't receive me: either because they were distracted, scared, too cautious to allow themselves to be vulnerable, or any other number of reasons. In those times, I felt cut off from the vine: isolated and alone.

That wound sometimes causes me to retaliate. If I'm unaware of the movements in my heart, my instinct is to close it off and allow a dam of resentment, withdrawal, and unforgiveness to form stone by stone. Those times of sin were born out of a good desire to see and be seen. However, I chose, unknowingly at times, to react with vice instead of virtue. As I allow Jesus access to my heart, I begin to see that knowledge and action are intertwined and necessary. God has provided remedies for both. He gives us knowledge that will help us know how to act—within our hearts and within Creation itself.

Moral Law

I recently taught fourth graders how God established the laws of Creation. God created the universe and every living creature to live and work in harmony: this is called Divine Law. Within Divine Law, God constructed Mathematical Laws and Scientific Laws.

To explain this to the students, I wrote a mathematical expression on the whiteboard and asked the fourth graders to solve it. They all excitedly arrived at the correct answer using PEMDAS—Mathematical Law. When I asked what would happen if I dropped my textbook to the ground—they gasped in glee when the book crashed to the floor, and all replied correctly that gravity would make it fall to the ground—Scientific Law.

God also constructed Moral Laws which can be understood with human reason. I used a somewhat silly example in class to describe Natural Moral Law vs. Revealed Moral Law. I asked the students, "would it be right or wrong to push a little old lady to the ground?" Their exuberant exclamation of "WRONG, so wrong!" exemplified that even young children understand God has written His law on their hearts.

CCC 1954 explains:

> **1954** The natural law is written and engraved in the soul of each and every man, because it is human reasoning ordaining him to do good and forbidding him to sin...

Even as children, we innately know right from wrong: that is natural law. However, even though man is ordained to do good, our hearts have been hardened through sin. That is why God also gives us Revealed Law.

Revealed Law goes deeper. It is especially helpful when the truths known by faith go beyond our reason. This is best exemplified in Matthew 5:43, "You have heard that it was said, 'You shall love your neighbor and hate your enemy.' But I say to you, love your enemies, and pray for those who persecute you.'" This higher law leads us not only to perfect happiness in Heaven beyond our human capabilities and understanding, but happiness here on earth as well.

The Old Law and the New Law

That launches us to the concept of the Old Law versus the New Law. As we study Scripture, we understand how from the beginning of time, God has worked through a covenant relationship to bring about our salvation. From our first parents, Adam and Eve, through the passing down of blessing and covenantal promises to Noah, Abraham, Moses, David and ultimately Jesus, we see God's law and love unfolded and unveiled. Paragraph 1961 in the *Catechism of the Catholic Church*, reminds us that God revealed His Law to Israel as a preparation for Christ's coming. It also *"expresses many truths accessible to reason."*

Stated in another way, the Ten Commandments are revealed aspects of the natural law. The Old Law is the first stage of revealed law.

CCC 1962 expounds:

> **1962** The Old Law is the first stage of revealed Law. Its moral prescriptions are summed up in the Ten Commandments. The precepts of the Decalogue lay the foundations for the vocation of man fashioned in the image of God; they prohibit what is contrary to the love of God and neighbor and prescribe what is essential to it. The Decalogue is a light offered to the conscience of every man to make God's call and ways known to him and to protect him against evil:
>
> God wrote on the tables of the Law what men did not read in their hearts.

What this paragraph conveys is that the Old Law (the Ten Commandments) is the first step of God teaching us. God must establish and reveal Justice before He reveals Mercy: otherwise, it just doesn't make sense. There is no need for mercy if there has been no injustice. It only makes sense for me to apologize to my friend if I had actually acted wrongly against her. It makes no sense for me to apologize to my friend for eating her piece of cake if there was no basis defining that as a problem or wrongdoing.

The law is a fatherly instruction by God. God desires and instructs us about the good because we flourish when we choose the good. In my family, if all of us consistently choose the good, we collectively operate in harmony—and it is literally heaven on earth! When any one of us goes against the good, conflict arises.

The Old Law was the first step in God revealing Himself to His people. The New Law, established through the Incarnation of Jesus to the world and fully revealed as His truth through the Gospels, is the fulfillment and full revelation of God. In Jesus and the Gospel message, we are given the power to fulfill what is asked of us in the Old Law.

When I think of the process of rearing my kids and the various stages of discipline and instruction, it is modeled after God's design, although I certainly didn't recognize it at the time. The first time my toddler attempted to dart into the street to chase a ball, my response was a quick, short, command, "Stop! Don't go into the street!"

I commanded his attention, avoided any possible tragic accidents, and pulled him to safety. It was then that I explained the dangers of darting into the street. As I'm sure anyone else who has ever parented a two-year-old, the next time his ball went into the street, this process was repeated. That is because he was simply too young to take in all that information at the tender age of two.

However, as he grew older and was able to receive and understand more complex information, I offered more elaborate instructions like, "we always have to look both ways, left and right, and back again, to make sure that there are no cars coming." The foundational principle was the same, I desired his safety, but instructions and explanations were different based on his maturity and responsibility.

The Old Law was given to humanity when we were like toddlers just beginning to learn how to follow God. Understanding and abiding in the Ten Commandments is one of the first steps we must take in our relationship with God and others. This is the foundation to living a life in the Spirit. Knowing and living the Ten Commandments fashions us into the most permeable vessels to receive and act upon His grace.

As humanity matures, God continues to expand and deepen our understanding and responsibility. The Old Law says, "thou shall not kill," but the New Law says, "I say to you, whoever is angry with his brother will be liable to judgment..." (Matthew 5:22). The New Law demands much more than the Old, yet I dare say its rewards are much greater as well. It requires us to love God as the center of all that we are, all that we have, and all that we do. The only means possible to answer this high call is through the power of the Holy Spirit, which we are given through our Baptism.

Sin and the Body of Christ

So often, we are tempted to view sin as one-sided. We forget the fact that no sin is private. Each and every sin, while perhaps personal, affects the entire body of Christ. Every time someone sins, private or not, someone is hurt.

A life lived grafted to the true vine broadens our understanding so that we don't just blindly or begrudgingly obey the motherly instruction "don't go into the street." Rather, we are given the wisdom and compassion to see the bigger picture.

In the running into the street example, we see that the Lord loves that child's life. God also puts on display how much He loves the mother who wants to protect her son. He knows she would be devastated if tragedy were to happen to him. Thirdly, we see how much the Lord loves the unsuspecting driver. God knows their life would be forever changed if involved in a tragic accident. We can see the ripple effect of each of our choices.

We are truly our brothers' keepers. We are the body of Christ and when one suffers, we all suffer. When one is loved, we are all loved. When one is shown mercy, we are all shown mercy.

But this is no pie-in-the-sky, easy task that can come with a lackadaisical attitude. Quite conversely, we must be vigilant and sharp. We must inform ourselves about God and His loving guidance for us. We must approach Him as humble children knowing that we have a good Father who created us and wants the best for us.

We must approach Him in acceptance of our dependence on Him. We must come with a coachable and docile heart. As Isaiah 55:8-9 reminds us, we must acknowledge that God's ways and thoughts are above ours. We must come with the trust and faith that He knows everyone's hearts, hurts, motivations, and then works simultaneously to usher in the goodness He created us for.

This takes a relationship. This takes conversation. This takes prayer. This takes a sacramental life. This takes humility to receive a free and powerful gift (God's grace) as well as a willingness to use it for its expressed intent.

Saint Pope John Paul II reminds us of our universal call to holiness.[6] Simply put, we are all called to be holy. Now, this is not some serene, never ruffled, non-emotional, robotic existence. It is actually quite the contrary. It is the lived experience to choose the good, to choose mercy, to choose love, oftentimes in spite of injustices. Then, with a determined heart and mind, we develop those relationships, repair the brokenness, and try again.

As CCC 418 reminds us, "As a result of original sin, human nature is weakened in its powers, subject to ignorance, suffering and the domination of death, and inclined to sin (this inclination is called "concupiscence")." Instead of feeling defeated by this reality, Venerable Bruno Lanteri's phrase *"nunc coepi"* which means "now I begin"[7] brings me much hope!

The fact is, we will fall into sin. But we get up again to learn, grow, and accept our weaknesses with a peaceful heart. We can do this because we know that behind our sin, God is there and wants to illuminate the why. He wants to take us into deeper healing, awareness, and relationship with Him and others. We are invited to confidently ask the Lord to come into all of those places of sin to teach, heal, and strengthen us.

Sin Leads to More Sin

Sin is tricky because it creates a proclivity to sin. When I make certain choices, it makes other choices either more difficult or easier the next time. This is sometimes referred to as the truth of cause and effect.

6 https://www.vatican.va/content/john-paul-ii/en/apost_exhortations/documents/hf_jp-ii_exh_30121988_christifideles-laici.html

7 https://www.omvusa.org/bruno-lanteri/about-bruno-lanteri/spirituality/nunc-coepi/#:~:text=Venerable%20Lanteri%20taught%20the%20importance,Coepi%2C%20Now%20I%20Begin.%E2%80%9D

When my son was a pre-teen, he and a group of boys realized that everyone in the class had the same password. Of course, the teachers had either explicitly or at least implicitly made it known that you were to only ever access your own account. However, this group of boys decided it would be fun to log into their friends' accounts and change the backgrounds on their friends' profiles. In one sense, it was a relatively harmless offense, but just like small sins, these choices can certainly lead to greater, more destructive ones in the future.

I was so thankful that my son came home and told me what happened. I was also thankful his teacher shared my desire to utilize this as a teaching moment, and enforced a punishment of no technology access in the classroom for a week as a consequence of his choice. When my son and I discussed the event, the Lord impressed upon my heart to walk through some logic with him.

He was certainly faced with a choice. There was peer pressure involved. There was weighing the probability of being caught. There was an assessment of the severity of the wrongdoing. Together, we acknowledged all these factors were real contributors to his decision-making process and carried weight. Middle school is a time of immense self-discovery and being influenced by what people think and say about you.

Bearing in mind a middle school mentality, we walked through a simple thought exercise together:

> Son, we saw the result of what happened with the choice you made. Let's look at what may have happened if you had instead chosen to not disobey (sin) and tell them, 'Nope guys, I'm not doing it.'
>
> Your friends may have called you a coward. They may have called you boring or a suck-up. Your friends may have said, yea, you're no fun: a real buzzkill. It would have taken a lot of courage to withstand those assaults from your friends. I also feel certain that if you said no, and withstood this test and trial, they wouldn't ask you to disobey the next time...why?

> Because kids are smart, constantly testing boundaries and looking to see how far people will let them go. By choosing to do the right thing and endure the mocking this time around, it becomes easier to tell them 'no' the next time.
>
> Here's why. Next time, they likely won't even ask you or invite you into their antics. Why? Because when given a choice to disobey a 'less dangerous' rule, you chose to instead obey. They won't invite a potential 'tattletale' into their escapades. So not only in the scenario did you choose virtue, but you also protected yourself from future temptations. Since you chose virtue this time it made your future-self less susceptible to temptation, and it simultaneously strengthened your virtue muscle.

I stopped and took a moment to let the silence linger in the air for a bit. Time stood still as I held my breath waiting for my son's response.

He looked me straight in the eye and said, "Mom, that makes a lot of sense. Thank you for telling me this: I see the wisdom in it." Any parents out there can feel the ribbon of relief that swelled through my heart with his sweet words and acknowledgement of truth. Truth always prevails. Sometimes we must remind each other by walking through these thought exercises together.

Sin tends to reproduce and reinforce itself. It clouds our conscience. We can easily convince ourselves that sin isn't sin.

My son easily could have convinced himself that because the school gave everyone the same password, it wasn't really a violation to go into another student's account. After all, if the administration thought it was a serious problem to hack into other students' accounts, they should have made the passwords more secure.

This mindset simply sidesteps the issue of personal responsibility for integrity and justice. Just because it was easy to violate someone's privacy, certainly doesn't make it right.

It's so obvious how in our fallen nature, justification to sin can slip in so easily. The slope of sin is extremely slippery. Many of us slide on that slope like black ice on the road. Not because we are bad people—but because we've momentarily forgotten that it rained overnight, the temperatures dipped below freezing, and our thoughts are consumed by the distractions and events of the day—forgetting about the real possibility that black ice has formed. We must be aware and vigilant, or all too easily, we can slip on this black ice of sin unsuspectingly.

Mortal Sin and Venial Sin

An important aspect of sin to consider is the degree of destruction the sin can produce in our hearts. CCC 1854 and 1855 define the Church's stance on the gravity of sin:

> **1854** Sins are rightly evaluated according to their gravity. The distinction between mortal and venial sin, already evident in Scripture, became part of the tradition of the Church. It is corroborated by human experience.
>
> **1855** Mortal sin destroys charity in the heart of man by a grave violation of God's law; it turns man away from God, who is his ultimate end and his beatitude, by preferring an inferior good to him. Venial sin allows charity to subsist, even though it offends and wounds it.

In other words, mortal sins destroy our relationship with God. We actively choose to turn our back on Him. We close the door to His grace. Venial sins on the other hand, weaken us but don't sever the relationship with God.

Read CCC 1856-1864 to better understand the nuances of these classifications of sin. CCC 1857 clearly states the requirements to be classified as mortal sin, "For a sin to be mortal, three conditions must together be met: Mortal sin is sin whose object is grave matter and which is also committed with full knowledge and deliberate consent."

It is important to keep in mind that when we understand the gravity and classification of our sin, it assists us in remedying our choice accordingly. Mortal sins brought with contrition to the Sacrament of Reconciliation receive God's abundant mercy, forgiveness, and restoration of grace to our souls.

Venial sins are forgiven during the Penitential Rite and with the reception of communion at Mass. CCC 1394 states, "As bodily nourishment stores lost strength, so the Eucharist strengthens our charity, which tends to be weakened in daily life; and this living charity *wipes away venial sins*."[8] Father Edward McNamara confirmed, "Since participation in Mass is infinitely the greatest form of reparatory and intercessory prayer that a human being can undertake, it is clear that his or her venial sins are likewise forgiven during Mass."[9]

In addition to the freedom that comes from the remission of venial sins during Mass, regular visits to the Sacrament of Reconciliation with both our mortal and venial sins assist us in accountability and our spiritual growth.

The footnote commentary on Psalm 51 offers a beautiful reflection on why it is important to have awareness of our sins.

> A lament, the most famous of the seven Penitential Psalms, prays for the removal of the personal and social disorders that sin has brought. The first part asks for deliverance from sin, not just as a past act but its emotional, physical, and social consequences. The second part seeks something more profound than wiping the slate clean: nearness to God, living by the spirit of God, like the relation between God and people described in Jeremiah 31:33-34. Nearness to God brings joy and the authority to teach sinners. Such proclamation is better than offering sacrifice. The last two verses express the hope that God's good will towards those who are cleansed and contrite will prompt Him to look favorably on the acts of worship offered in the Jerusalem Temple.[10]

8 https://www.catholiccrossreference.online/catechism/#!/search/1394

9 https://www.ewtn.com/catholicism/library/efficacy-of-the-penitential-rite-4954

10 https://bible.usccb.org/bible/psalms/51

Guilt vs. Shame

A very important aspect to bring to light when we talk about sin is the distinct difference between guilt and shame. Guilt acknowledges and takes accountability for our sins. It pricks our conscience and encourages us to repent. Shame condemns us and freezes us in a false identity statement. It discourages us from seeking and receiving God's mercy.

So how do we know whose voice we hear? Fr. Mark Toups recounts that his spiritual director gave him incredible insight in the year leading up to his ordination.

> Fr. H helped me see how both the devil and the Lord might be using the same words but were not saying the same thing...the enemy would whisper, 'You cannot do this. You will always need help.' These words made me feel unworthy. I felt accused. I felt condemned. I thought, 'I cannot do this. I will never be able to do this.' Notice that when the enemy spoke those words, I focused on what I could not do. In contrast, in moments of prayer Jesus would gently say, 'you cannot do this, you will always need help.' These same words, because of who said them, felt different. I thought 'That's right. I can't do this. But then again, who can? I'll always need help, so Jesus please help me.' Notice that when Jesus spoke the same words, they made me aware of what he could do in me.[11]

The Lord convicts. The devil condemns. "For God did not send his Son into the world to condemn the world, but that the world might be saved through him" (John 3:17).

The devil will taunt you through shame about your sin. He attempts to convince you that you are beyond redemption and saving. He will tempt you to believe you are too far gone to ask for forgiveness and not worthy to be forgiven. If you have any of the following thoughts—"no, I'm not going to pray," "no, I'm not going to Confession," "it's not that big of a deal; I can just ignore this," or "I'm too far gone, why even bother trying to ask for help" you can confidently declare it is the voice of the evil one. We must boldly reject his lies.

---

11 Fr. Mark Toups. *The Ascension Lenten Companion Year C.* Ascension Publishing Group, LLC. 2022.

God will lovingly bring your sins to your awareness inviting you to choose forgiveness and redemption. The story of the woman at the well (John 4:1-42), is an incredible testimony of the transforming power of Jesus. In the story, Jesus asks the woman about her husband. This calls to mind her sin. What was her response? Through a series of questions and answers, she came to know Him as the Messiah. The woman, now full of freedom from forgiveness declares, "Come see a man who told me everything I have done."

Just like the woman at the well experienced, encounters with Jesus reveal to us that our past does not define our future nor our potential. Jesus loves us enough to help us recognize when we have chosen a lesser good. He loves us and wants to heal us. Encounters with Jesus lead to profound transformation and a new sense of purpose.

The Commandments Are a Gift

This is the beauty of the Commandments. They bring to our consciousness the cosmic reality in which we live. They are given to us as a gift to inform us of the powerful ways God invites us to cooperate with Him in His saving work.

CCC 396 states:

> **396** God created man in his image and established him in his friendship. A spiritual creature, man can live this friendship only in free submission to God. The prohibition against eating "of the tree of the knowledge of good and evil" spells this out: "for in the day that you eat of it, you shall die." The "tree of the knowledge of good and evil" symbolically evokes the insurmountable limits that man, being a creature, must freely recognize and respect with trust. Man is dependent on his Creator, and subject to the laws of creation and to the moral norms that govern the use of freedom.

I encourage you to read the entire section (CCC 396-401) on The Fall because there is so much to chew on, however for the sake of brevity, I'll share how this one paragraph has changed my daily life and perspective.

Having this knowledge about God's Providence and Supremacy means I have to freely and fully accept that God is God and I am not. I have to freely allow myself to be in friendship with Him. If I merely "go through the motions" to enter into a friendship because it's something I'm told I "should do," it will never be a fully realized friendship and relationship. It will always lack intimacy and trust because I haven't given fully and freely, even though certainly God has.

This concept can perhaps be more fully understood from a parenting perspective. As parents we are wise to guard against the mentality of "because I said so." It is a dangerous and ultimately limited method of parenting. While it is true that my husband and I hold knowledge, wisdom, experience, and authority over our children (just like God does over me), when we do not establish an environment and allow our children to enter into friendship freely with us, there will be a limited and authoritative relationship versus one that offers love freely given and received.

To go a step further, certainly I can 'force' my children's obedience. However, any of you that have tried this methodology usually see the rebellion begin around the pre-teen or teenage years. Children instinctively understand they do not have the financial and other means to go out independently so they begrudgingly, defiantly, or silently and resentfully obey until the moment they hit an age where they can flee from the perceived oppression. I've watched many parents employ this style, not necessarily intentionally, but simply because they weren't taught another way.

By God's grace I knew that there was no way my husband and I would know how to handle every situation with our kids. I knew that we both experienced things in our own childhoods that we didn't want to emulate. Realistically, the chances were high that we would, even if unknowingly, bring those habits to the table. So we turned to God and asked Him to show us how to parent. This extraordinary First Commandment was the foundation.

The Commandments are how God reveals Himself and His love to guide us in our lives. So with this mindset, instead of being authoritative, we have intentionally taught God's word and His truth to our children. We try our best, despite our flawed and weak ability, to let it govern and direct all of our parenting.

My kids learn that they too have limits: that for a time, they must recognize and respect with trust. It has been many a conversation in our household that our expectation of obedience isn't out of some desire for control or pride. Rather God has put us as Mom and Dad in a place of authority to teach and give them opportunities to practice obedience to us. This practice in obedience to us ultimately translates to obedience to God.

God is invisible, but as parents, we are His visible participants to help our children to come to know and love Him. The more that my husband and I can create an environment similar to the original paradise in which our children feel safe to trust us, and thereby God, we can do our part to help foster their (and our own) deeper relationship with Him. We'll delve further into this huge responsibility we have as parents toward our children's salvation as they grow in Christian maturity as young adults in the Fourth Commandment. But suffice to say, as parents we are given the gift and responsibility to reveal the Father's love to our children in word and action.

The true gift of the Commandments is that it is God revealing Himself, His heart, and His holy will to us. As we take a deeper look at these Commandments, I invite you to view each Commandment in that light. Challenge yourself to view the command as a whisper of love from the Father to your heart instead of a restriction meant to limit you. View it as a conversation with a close friend who wants you to see them and be received in love by you, and equally, to see you and receive you in their loving embrace.

CHAPTER ONE

The First Commandment—You Shall Have No Other Gods Before Me

Many hearts rear back in pride and indignation in response to this First Commandment. "How egotistical and demanding for God to command this!"

Lucifer's rebellion was the first sin that occurred in Creation when he declared 'he would not serve.'[12] It is understood that angels are not subject to the same limitations as man. They have greater wisdom and power than man. Angels are pure intellect. However, even with full knowledge of the eternal consequence that awaited them by turning away from God, Revelation 12:4 states that a third of the angels were swept from the Heavens.

Satan's pride was his downfall.[13] We must absolutely be on guard for this dangerous and devastating sin. It can cost us our eternal happiness. This is because the First Commandment flies in the face

12 https://www.oursundayvisitor.com/is-satans-vow-to-not-serve-in-the-bible/

13 https://www.newadvent.org/summa/1063.htm

of two powerful temptations: human pride and self-sufficiency. Due to original sin we have a natural tendency to indulge in these two temptations and it can be exacerbated by our lived experiences. When viewed from a worldly lens of dominance and pride, the First Commandment seems repulsive.

It is easy to understand why so many come to this unfortunate conclusion. Many people do not experience a childhood that is reminiscent of God's fatherhood. Often families are wrought with some level of dysfunction that leaves children who grow into adults with an inaccurate or inadequate view of God. This creates many internal insecurities that push us towards human pride and self-sufficiency to survive. Many then continue to allow pride to steer their minds and wills and thus promote this distorted view of God. We don't have to look too far to see that this is true for so many people—perhaps even in our own hearts.

Yet, the Lord knows everything. He is ever merciful and patient with us. He steadfastly loves us and continues to reveal Himself to us; especially when we ask and allow Him to do so.

In my many years of ministry, I have found misunderstandings about this Commandment are usually not an intentional disregard for it, but rather a lack of intentional focus. My prayer is that you will allow the Lord primacy in your heart and mind. The First Commandment serves to prepare our hearts to receive God as He unveils His heart to us.

When it is viewed from God's loving care for us, the First Commandment is prudent and respects our dignity. It establishes the premier way for us to render justice to Him. God is the Creator of everything. If we are one with Him through obedience, He will take care of everything. As our loving Father, it places us in an environment to trust in His all powerful knowledge. This trust allows and inspires humans to develop into the beautiful people He created us to be from the beginning of time.

It is a mutually loving relationship that fosters trust, proper order, and safeguards against the many temptations and vices we are guaranteed to encounter. Like a good mother protects her toddler from recklessly crossing the street, God gives us the Commandments for our safety. Like that toddler who must obey his mother to be safe from passing cars, obedience is necessary for us to flourish as children of God.

Faith, Hope, and Love

Let's dive a bit deeper into the specifics of this First Commandment.

I love the eloquence and beauty of CCC 2086 and encourage you to read it now.This paragraph outlines the three theological virtues: faith, hope and love. I remember these three words inscribed on one of my most favorite James Avery rings that I wore in middle school. I'd like to say it was my favorite because I understood the virtues described. In all honesty though, it was simply because it sounded and looked nice in its uniform silver lettering. I actually had no idea about the depth and importance of these three words.

These three virtues dispose us to live in a relationship with the Holy Trinity. Their motive, origin, and object is God Himself. Said in another way, these are the three essential God-given virtues that are infused into us at Baptism. Our proper response to these gifts would be to ask for, develop, and operate from and with them during our journey with God. These theological virtues outline for us how to choose to know and love God.

To more fully appreciate how the Church defines faith, please read CCC 153-164 now. In layman's terms, faith is a determined trust and commitment to give oneself entirely to God. It means we maintain an openness and trust in Him. Even if we struggle to understand His ways, we struggle as someone who trusts Him.

I draw a parallel to my earthly father here. There were many times in my childhood that I questioned and didn't like rules my dad required and enforced. Be that as it may, most of the time I trusted his love and wisdom enough to say, "Dad, I don't like this, I don't want this, but I have faith knowing that you know better than I and you want what is best for me." It can be the same for us with faith in God.

CCC 1817-1818 expounds upon the virtue of hope. Please read them now. Hope trusts that there is something greater than the finite life lived here on earth. It is a deep internal desire to live this earthly life with an eye for eternal life and happiness with God in Heaven.

We need hope. Hope protects us from discouragement and selfishness. If we place our hope in God's promises, we are free to love the people around us and endure all circumstances because we know that God is faithful.

My mind swirls with all of the disappointments, pain, and suffering I have encountered in my own life as well as countless stories people have shared with me along the way. There is real pain, injustice, and suffering in this world. Without hope in God's promises, it can be so tempting to give up and succumb to the temptation that this is all the darkened world has to offer. Hope purifies and transforms the desires we have to act and live for God. It gives us the motivation and power to know there is something greater than the present darkness. In trust and power we get to actively live and fight for eternal glory.

Finally, we have the greatest of these theological virtues: love. This virtue is to love God above all things for His own sake and to love our neighbor as ourselves. Love has to be translated into action; it is more than merely feelings. Many great authors have lamented how in the English language we have only one word to describe different types of love. I love chocolate cake. I love my husband. I love the beauty of a gorgeous sunset with the soft rustling of leaves on a warm spring night. Each of these statements are true, yet they are incredibly different in emotion and call to action. The kind of love we mean here is selfless love.

My favorite definition of love is to will the good of another person. To love in this way takes courage, self-reflection, and the power and guidance of the Holy Spirit. And, if that happens to swell your heart to do so, great! From my own struggle, it certainly sounds a lot easier than what is actually done! To actively and consistently choose love is only possible with the power of the Holy Spirit.

Since these theological virtues are so critical to understand, appreciate, and obey God's First Commandment, we need to highlight the ways we can sin against them.

Sins Against Faith

The various ways we can sin against faith are voluntary doubt, involuntary doubt, incredulity, heresy, apostasy, and schism. Open your *Catechism* and read paragraphs 2088-2089 to help explain these terms.

It wasn't until I was well into my adult life that I even realized the above mentioned were sins. This realization splashed my face with chilling water. It is tough to hold yourself to high standards. In fact, it can only be done with God's grace as quoted in Philippians 4:13, "I have strength for everything through Him who empowers me." But the gain of a life lived in greater harmony with God and others is more than worth the struggle.

For me, involuntary doubt, left unchecked and without the pursuit of intentional learning the why of Church teaching, caused a lot of internal strife and cognitive dissonance. Looking back, I can recognize how I struggled with this sin of involuntary doubt when it came to the topic of abortion in my high school and college years.

I had a notion about what the Church taught, but I avoided delving into the subject matter to inform my conscience. Instead, I chose to passively accept opinions and persuasive arguments. There is purpose in the struggle to truly understand what God, through His Church, teaches. Instead of thrusting myself into wrestling with this controversial topic, I sinned via involuntary doubt, and only managed a half-hearted attempt to be compassionate to friends who faced these devastating situations. When I chose not to invest in learning what the Church teaches, not only did I sin against God, I also wasn't authentically compassionate to my friends in need.

Compassion is defined as suffering with another and thereby feeling compelled to take action.[14] True compassion is a powerful force for good. It compels us to connect with others to make a positive impact in their lives. If love means willing the genuine best good for another, then true compassion is fully exemplified when we understand their suffering within the fullest context of God's love.

Before humbly seeking God and the reasons behind His Commandments, I failed on both sides. Not only did I lack in truth, but I also was unable to truly be compassionate. When I took the time to wrestle with Church teaching it actually broadened my capacity for love in word and action for my brothers and sisters who are faced with unwanted pregnancies.

It allowed me to enter into and understand the depth of their suffering and wounded hearts beyond the external situation. By better understanding God's desire for each of us to live a life filled with dignity for the whole human person, I better understood the depth of the battle they faced emotionally, spiritually, and physically.

The gift of the Commandments increased both my sense of commitment to value all human life and protect the most vulnerable, as well as my love, compassion, and active work to help support both mom, dad, and child.

Specifically, in recent years a group of parishioners have actively worked within our diocese to compile and communicate all the resources that are available to help families in need.[15] But even more importantly, wrestling through this sin of involuntary doubt about a specific Church teaching has greatly enabled me to compassionately and lovingly walk alongside these friends with hope. Now I can not only meet them in their temporal needs but I can better accompany them through the emotional and spiritual healing process as well.

---

14 https://www.catholicnewsagency.com/column/52255/compassion-pity-mercy

15 https://gscc.net/walking-with-moms-in-need/

I pray this example invites you to think about the ways you may have sinned against faith. Pray with me: *Holy Spirit, convict my heart. Help me to see that you are the fullest expression of love.*

The gift of faith is of primary importance to navigate our world and our relationships authentically. There is no condemnation to admit our shortcomings and failures. The truth is when I admit and repent of my failures, God stands with His open arms of mercy embracing me in His forgiveness and love. Romans 5:20 declares God's truth, "The law entered in so that transgression might increase but, where sin increased, grace overflowed all the more." Jesus has come to save us from our sins and intercede on our behalf to the Father and live our fullest life.

Sins Against Hope

Despair and presumption are sins against hope. Open your *Catechism* to read paragraph 2091 for the Church's definition of despair.

Despair, in a nutshell, is when all hope to believe or receive God's mercy and forgiveness is lost. Mark 3:29 calls to mind this sin, "But whoever blasphemes against the holy Spirit will never have forgiveness, but is guilty of an everlasting sin." This is such a devastating sin because it believes a lie spoken from the evil one. He tempts us to sin at every turn, and once we fall to temptation, the evil one tries to convince us what we have done is too bad to ever be forgiven or overcome. On the contrary, Jesus' mercy is so full and complete.

We must be on guard against this sin of despair and always combat it with the truth. The only sin that isn't forgiven is the one we don't ask forgiveness for. Every contrite humble request for forgiveness and act of repentance is embraced and bathed in God's love and mercy.

Read CCC 2092. There are two kinds of presumption: man presuming upon his own capacities and man presuming upon God's almighty power or His mercy. These sins are again all too common. Most of us don't pause long enough to consider we have committed them. These sins, like so many others, can slowly seep into our consciousness unnoticed until they are pointed out to us.

A dear friend of mine has struggled in a new phase in his life. After his wife died, he had to navigate roads he hadn't journeyed before. I recall a conversation we had early on in his "new normal" where I was solely there to listen. I remember when he spoke the words, "Jesus knows my heart," my heart lit a flame. I knew it burned because my friend was operating outside of God's Commandments in some of his choices. The Holy Spirit immediately alerted my heart to the presumption in my friend's attitude: "God knows my heart and therefore I can do what I want and what feels right. God will understand and look the other way."

This friend planned to continue in his choices, even with the knowledge that they were against God's commands. He presumed God's mercy to obtain His forgiveness without conversion, and glory without merit. This is a difficult pill to swallow; both for me and my friend. After that conversation, I prayed daily for a few months for his heart to be opened and convicted. Sure enough, within a few months the Lord convicted my heart that I needed to speak some decidedly direct and bold words to my friend. I was so scared. I was scared that he wouldn't receive me. I was afraid he would walk away from our friendship. I was afraid of all the bad things he would think of me. But I also knew the Lord initiated me to take this leap of courage.

I invited him to consider his situation. I invited him to repent of his actions and allow me to accompany him with loving support along this difficult journey to deny pleasures for a greater good. He looked me straight in the eye and said he couldn't do it. The ask was too much. I could understand. I hugged him. I continued to pray and the Lord invited me to fast on his behalf. I am terrible at fasting and fail virtually every time I try.

That failure to be able to fast on his behalf was such a gift to me. To fail right alongside my friend in our attempts to grow in holiness increased my compassion and commitment to persevere. That friend still persists in his ways, but I also persist in prayer and fasting for him. I love him dearly. I love his willingness to allow me to speak those frightful words and not turn me away. I will continue to love him, hopefully right into our loving Father's arms.

Through our baptism we are infused with the virtue of hope. We ourselves, or through our friendships, will be faced with many opportunities to sin against hope. What a gift you can offer when you recognize a friend's battle with despair or presumption. You can offer your encouragement, prayer, and guidance as a display and witness of your love for them. We also can foster and pray in gratitude when our friends hold us accountable and intercede for us when we need help.

Sins Against Love

The ways we can sin against the theological virtue of love are defined in CCC 2094. Of these sins I want to address hatred of God because in many ways I think we might be surprised about this sin.

Hatred of God is a prevalent sentiment in America that has been adopted by many. It is borne out of pride and denies God's goodness. It is an errant sentiment that accuses God of taking all the fun out of life and labels Him as a tyrant who inflicts punishments upon us for our wrongdoings. This sentiment is so common yet so disastrous and perhaps one of the biggest lies of the evil one. Ironically, the Lord, as He does so often in my life, provided a unique experience as I was writing this section.

On a dreary, rainy day, I took the kids to the local arcade where I wrote while they played. An older gentleman approached me and asked if I was a student. My middle-aged self laughed at the absurdity of the comment, but it opened the door to a conversation with this man. I took my earbuds out to give him my full attention. In the 5-10 minute conversation that followed, he told me he had an unforgettable encounter with Jesus shortly after he was diagnosed with terminal cancer.

In his vision, a 60 foot tall Jesus entered into his hospital room, bent down, and cradled this man into His arms. He was miraculously cured shortly afterwards. In the middle of an arcade, this man spilled his heart out to me. He spoke about his poor choices in his youth. He chose to marry, in his words, 'the easiest girl in school.' He expressed his sadness that his children have followed in his well-worn pattern of addiction to drugs and alcohol. One of the striking things this man said after he told me of His encounter with Jesus, was that "so many people think God is there to remove all fun and then hold it over their heads when they do wrong...that's not how He is at all."

There stood a man before me nearing the end of his life. He felt compelled to share some of his life stories with a total stranger. He articulated how finally after so many years of doing things his way, how after viewing God and His Commandments erroneously, he has realized God's abundant love and mercy. He wants his children, his grandchildren, and complete strangers to learn and accept the truth much sooner than he did.

These sins against the theological virtues highlight the ways we are invited to know and love God. We always have a choice; that is the gift of free will. Knowing and loving God is the first part of this Commandment. The next question is, rooted in our knowledge and love of God, how will we worship and serve Him?

Worship and Serve God

Next we will move to the second half of the Commandment, "only Him you shall worship and serve." Knowing how and why we are called to worship and serve God and God alone is important to highlight. Having a solid understanding can help us identify those ways we unknowingly fall short. Identifying our shortcomings is not for condemnation. It is an invitation to acknowledge that the Lord passionately pursues us and our hearts. He desires to give us a joy-filled life beyond all understanding.

To adore God is to acknowledge, in respect and absolute submission, the nothingness of the creature who would not exist but for God. The worship of the one God sets man free from turning in on himself, from the slavery of sin and the idolatry of the world.

There have been too many times to count where worshipping and serving God has saved me from turning in on myself and becoming enslaved to sin. How do we serve God? Matthew 25:37-40 reminds us. "Then the righteous will answer him and say, 'Lord, when did we see you hungry and feed you, or thirsty and give you drink? When did we see you a stranger and welcome you, or naked and clothe you? When did we see you ill or in prison, and visit you?' And the king will say to them in reply, 'Amen, I say to you, whatever you did for one of these least brothers of mine, you did for me.'" Serving God oftentimes is experienced in the manner and ways we serve each other.

Marriage is one of the noticeably tangible ways we live out our call to serve God. As I'm sure you can imagine and perhaps experienced yourself, there have been many times of trouble and conflict throughout my own married life. One of the really beautiful gifts we learned early on in our marriage was when we found ourselves in an argument, where we, in our spiritually immature selves, viewed the other as the enemy, we stopped and went outside of ourselves and served. Yes, that means we went angry, continuing to yell in the car—still bound up in our emotions and hurt. Yet, we then stepped out of the car, took a deep breath, put a sometimes forced smile on our face, and walked into the community center doors to make peanut and butter sandwiches for the less fortunate.

Miracles happen when we choose to serve. Getting out of ourselves, refusing the opportunity to turn in on ourselves, we allowed the grace of the Lord, in serving His people, to fill us with love and light. All of a sudden, all the anger and ill will towards the other was lessened. That's not to say we didn't have real conversations and discussions afterwards to fix legitimate problems and concerns, but we allowed God's grace and mercy to fill our hearts instead of the slavery of sin.

You see, the Lord doesn't need us to serve Him because He needs something done. He's God, after all. He gives us the gift and command to serve Him because we need it to empty ourselves of the chains and bondage of sin and allow Him to fill us with His grace and love.

Ah, I love Him. He is so excessively good to us! Everything He does and commands is out of, and for Love, as He is Love Himself! He is the personification of love!

Sins Against Serving God Alone: Occult Practices

Let's tackle the ways we can commit sin against serving God and God alone. These first ones can be classified as the occult. Superstition, idolatry, divination, and magic are all ways that seem to be ever more present in this day and age. Open your *Catechism* and read paragraphs 2111 to 2117 for definitions of these sins.

All of these actions give power, honor, and/or reverence to something in place of God. For example, wearing a good luck charm can seem innocent enough, yet when you look at the motivation for doing so, you might be surprised to realize what this action really suggests. When you wear a good luck charm, you ask for and place your trust in an object to bring you what you desire. You do not direct your reverence and trust to God who knows you and all that you need. Matthew 6:7-8 reminds us, "In praying, do not babble like the pagans, who think that they will be heard because of their many words. Do not be like them. Your Father knows what you need before you ask Him."

At first, I might have been inclined to dismiss this section on the occult as irrelevant. Thankfully, before I even recognized the dangers of these sins against the First Commandment, I was given a huge gift. About fifteen years ago, I was an active member of a mom's group and one of our topics was on spiritual warfare. Now at this point in my spiritual journey, I knew surprisingly little about spiritual warfare. To be honest, much of it, even the name, scared me. However there was a woman who visited one of our meetings. She brought with her a book and handed it to me and said that I should probably read it. Since I'm a fairly open person, I took the book and cracked it open that same night. I cannot even remember the title nor the author of the book but I remember it shook me to my core. It was a story of a woman who had a high ranking position in a satanic cult. It told of her conversion story. When I read the section about occult activity, my life was forever changed.

The book spoke about repenting of any and all occult activity whether you knew it was a sin or not. At that moment, the Holy Spirit brought to my mind a time when I was a kid at a friend's slumber party. The friend brought out a ouija board and we played with it. I remember being a little uncomfortable, but it was all only for fun, no big deal. I don't recall anything ever happening; I don't think the board ever moved, and we moved on to other things.

Fast forward to reading this book in my room late at night. I was convicted to pray the prayer of repentance that was offered in the book. What happened next stopped me cold in my tracks. As soon as I completed the prayer, fire raged through my entire body. It started from the tips of my toes and every tiny cell in my body exploded with heat. The fire raced through all of my limbs, core, and out through the top of my head. At that moment I was completely terrified. Nothing like that had ever happened to me before. I put my rosary on top of the book until I dropped it off on the lady's porch as soon as the sun came up the next day.

This event was a huge point of conversion and grace in my life. My spiritual journey took on a new importance and intentionality that very day. Even though I did not know I had sinned against God all those years ago, I took ownership and responsibility to repent and make amends the moment I realized my actions were a sin. As I allowed myself to consider the ways I had unknowingly sinned against the Lord, He didn't punish me. Instead, He poured healing waters into my heart, and inspired me to seek Him out even more.

God poured His grace and mercy upon me. A part of my heart that I didn't even perceive was closed to Him through sin burst open. The floodgates of grace were unleashed. I felt such a sense of gratitude that He loved me so fully and rescued me from darkness. Even though it's hard to admit our failings, known and unknown, intentional and unintentional, it's worth it. I know how thankful I am that someone shared information about sins of the occult with me so I can more fully become who God had created and continually molds me to be.

Sins Against Serving God Alone: Irreligion, Atheism, and Agnosticism

As we continue to unpack the First Commandment, we will highlight Irreligion and Atheism and Agnosticism. Read paragraph 2118 in the *Catechism*.

Tempting God happens when we put His goodness and almighty power to the test by word or deed. We can recall how Satan tempted Jesus in the desert. "The challenge contained in such tempting of God wounds the respect and trust we owe our Creator and Lord. It always harbors doubt about His love, His providence, and His power" (CCC 2119). This can be an incredibly tricky sin especially when we find ourselves in desperate situations.

CCC 2120 and 2021 define sacrilege and simony. For example, this applies to charging a fee for any sacraments or Mass intentions. No one should ever be denied a sacrament due to their poverty. Stipends or gifts of gratitude can be given to our clergy, but payment is never to be required.

Next we define atheism in CCC 2124. Atheism, similar to hatred of God, seems to be especially prevalent in our time.

In many ways atheism is pretty self explanatory: it is when we simply dismiss the existence of God and thus all He commands and orchestrates. My assumption is that if you are reading this book, you are not likely committing sins of atheism in its strict sense. However, before we wipe our brow in relief, the *Catechism* is quick to challenge believers about our role in promoting atheism.

Read CCC 2125 to challenge yourself with its assertion.

With this in mind, we are invited to take a deep look at our lives. Do we truly witness to everyone around us by our words and lives that Jesus is real and our first priority? Do the people we encounter every day through work, soccer games, school, and even church secretly (or openly) wonder how despite the many circumstances we find ourselves, we carry ourselves with joy beyond all telling? Do they wonder what secret or knowledge we have that they want? If these answers are not a resounding yes, then offer a prayer to the Lord and ask for His grace to begin anew today and live like our faith makes a difference. It is the difference between death and life!

Finally, consider Agnosticism as a sin against the First Commandment. CCC 2127-2128 defines and clarifies agnosticism.

The good news is that if you have picked up this book, you are searching for God and definitely putting in effort towards knowing, loving, and serving Him!

Reflection Questions

Take some time to reflect upon the questions below. Consider writing in your Reconciliation journal or notebook of your choice. Invite the Lord to be present with you as you consider these questions.

- *What thoughts or feelings surfaced when reading this chapter?*
- *Did anything stand out to you as new or different than you had previously considered?*
- *Did the Lord convict your heart in a particular way?*
- *Are you moved to repent?*
- *Did you receive any interior movement in your heart, a consolation, or a deeper love for God or neighbor?*
- *What do you want to ask the Lord for now?*

Examination of Conscience—First Commandment

Now that we have explored the First Commandment, perhaps in greater detail than you have before, I invite you to sit with the Lord and review the following questions. What is He saying to you? Come, Holy Spirit, Come!

1. *Do I freely submit to God and acknowledge my dependence on Him?*
2. *Do I recognize and respect with trust that as a human, I have certain limitations?*
3. *Do I allow myself to be subject to God's laws of Creation and to moral norms that govern my use of freedom?*
4. *Do I accept God and worship Him?*

5. **Sins against Faith:**
   a. *Am I guilty of voluntary doubt—disregarding or refusing to hold as true what God has revealed and the Church proposes for belief?*
   b. *Am I guilty of involuntary doubt—hesitating in believing, difficulty in overcoming objections of the faith, or anxiety aroused by its obscurity?*
   c. *Am I guilty of incredulity—neglect of revealed truth or willful refusal to assent to it?*
   d. *Am I guilty of heresy—obstinate post-baptismal denial of truth or obstinate doubt?*
   e. *Am I guilty of apostasy—total repudiation of the Christian faith?*
   f. *Am I guilty of schism—refusal of submission to the Roman Pontiff or of communion with the members of the Church subject to him?*

6. **Sins against Hope:**
   a. *Am I guilty of despair about my salvation or the forgiveness of my sins?*
   b. *Am I guilty of presumption—have I presumed upon my own capacities, believing I can save myself without help from on high?*
   c. *Am I guilty of presumption—have I presumed upon God's almighty power or His mercy, hoping to obtain his forgiveness without conversion and glory without merit?*

7. **Sins against Love:**
   a. *Do I sin against love by indifference—neglecting or refusing to reflect on divine charity, denying its power?*
   b. *Do I sin against love by ingratitude—failing or refusing to acknowledge divine charity and to return Him love for love?*
   c. *Do I sin against love by lukewarmness—hesitation or negligence in responding to divine love and its promptings?*
   d. *Do I sin against love by acedia—refusing the joy that comes from God, or am I repelled by divine goodness?*

e. *Do I sin against love by hatred of God—coming from pride, do I deny God's goodness and instead think it a curse and view God as the one who forbids sins and inflicts punishments?*

8. *Am I guilty of superstition—attributing importance in some way magical to certain practices or attributing efficacy of prayers or of sacramental signs to their mere external performance, apart from the interior dispositions they demand?*

9. *Am I guilty of idolatry in any form; satanism, power, pleasure, race, ancestors, the state, money etc.?*

10. *Am I guilty of participating in occult activities; consulting horoscopes, astrology, ouija board, palm reading, interpretation of omens and lots, the phenomena of clairvoyance, recourse to mediums, or the practicing of magic or sorcery?*

11. *Am I guilty of tempting God, especially in times of extreme trial or suffering?*

12. *Am I guilty of sacrilege—profaning or treating unworthily the sacraments, liturgical actions, or persons, things, or places consecrated to God; especially the Eucharist?*

13. *Am I guilty of simony—buying or selling of spiritual things?*

14. *Am I guilty of atheism—rejecting or denying the existence of God?*

15. *Am I guilty of cultivating atheism in others—through practical materialism, atheistic humanism, or economic and social liberation? Am I careless about my instruction in the faith, presenting its teaching falsely, or failing in my religious, moral, or social life thereby concealing instead of revealing the true nature of God and religion?*

16. *Am I guilty of agnosticism—through making no judgment about God's existence, declaring it impossible to prove, or even affirm or deny?*

CHAPTER TWO

The Second Commandment—You Shall Not Take the Name of the Lord Your God in Vain

The Second Commandment is one of the more straightforward Commandments. Our names are incredibly powerful and rich in meaning. Our names are also deeply personal and intimate. Think of when someone says your name. The way they speak your name can evoke a myriad of emotions. I can say my children's names saturated with my love and tenderness, or I can say their name in frustration and anger. Depending on which way I speak their name, I can literally see the dramatically different effect on their spirit.

I love CCC 2144, "Respect for His name is an expression of the respect owed to the mystery of God himself and to the whole sacred reality it evokes." Fr. Jim Gigliotti, T.O.R. wrote:

> One piece of this Good News had the capacity to move me deeply and it went like this: When the Hebrew people spoke of GOD, the concept of pronouncing GOD was too sacred to verbalize. When

> writing about God or some revelation from God, some letters were used: 'YHWH.' Reading the WORD aloud, there was to be what seemed to be a second of silence at YHWH. We would later say 'Yahweh' but for the Jews, no! Instead, an almost imperceptible breath was taken. One would gently breathe in 'YAH' and breathe out 'WEH.' GOD was the BREATH of LIFE, too awesome, and greatly brilliant that if one were to ever SEE God, one knew one's life would be over. Human creatures could not sustain such dazzling omniscience.[16]

The Lord, our Creator, the great I AM, is so pure, so holy, the purest definition of love, that our only response is reverence and awe at His name. Christianity is the only religion that confesses a God that is so humble and intimate with us to share His name and His very self with us, especially in the Eucharist.

God reveals His Sacred name as Jesus. "Because of this, God greatly exalted him and bestowed on him the name that is above every name, that at the name of Jesus every knee should bend, of those in heaven and on earth and under the earth, and every tongue confess that Jesus Christ is Lord, to the glory of God the Father" (Phil 2:9-11). Jesus is present when we utter His name, and we ought to take the responsibility of venerating His name with the delicate care of a mosaic artist.

Blasphemy

The most obvious sin against this Second Commandment is profaning His name, otherwise known as blasphemy.

CCC 2148 offers a clear definition of blasphemy. Take a moment to read it now.

There it is in black and white: misusing the name of God is a grave sin. Oftentimes my children ask me, "Mom, what constitutes a grave sin?" Sometimes in my own limitations and blind spots, I can struggle

16 https://www.facebook.com/share/p/1W1Rbh9BQQ/

to answer that question. That is why I am so grateful that the Church gives us clear cut knowledge and instruction to help us. As we journey through the *Catechism*, grave sins are identified.

Fr. John Bartunek, LC offers clarity on what constitutes grave matter. He states,

> Whenever we choose something radically opposed to God's goodness – like murder, fornication, or refusing to praise and thank God by attending Sunday Mass – we are, basically, rejecting God's friendship. The object of our choice (the "matter" of the sin) is in direct and full opposition to the very heart of God. By choosing it, we are saying to God that we can live without him, that we don't want him around. In this way, we destroy the theological virtue of charity in our soul. That constitutes a mortal sin, which God will readily forgive if we sincerely repent and go to him in the sacrament of confession. Whenever we give in to temptations that are opposed to God's goodness in less radical ways – like sleeping in a little longer than necessary, eating a little more than is necessary, stealing small office supplies from an employer for personal use – we aren't outright severing our friendship with God, but we're distancing ourselves from him. These actions would not constitute grave matter. In these cases, we're making small concessions to selfishness that close off certain sectors of our heart from his love and thereby weaken the theological virtue of charity in our soul. That constitutes a venial sin, which God will readily forgive if we sincerely repent even if we don't go to confession, but which, if left unrepented, could easily snowball into the outright rebellion of mortal sin.[17]

While I am naturally an obedient person, I never really truly considered the magnitude of the Second Commandment. Our identity is in our name. God's identity is in His name. This Commandment goes much deeper than only something we say off-handedly. If you are like me and never really gave this Commandment too much thought, I invite you to stop here and ask the Lord to show you why He gave us this Commandment and how He is inviting you to respond. You might be surprised.

---

17 https://spiritualdirection.com/2011/08/22/what-constitutes-grave-sin-how-can-i-know-if-it-is-ok-to-receive-the-eucharist

I have four children and am readily involved in their daily activities. The amount of times I overhear "OMG" when I volunteer at their school is overwhelming. It is one concrete way that I have encouraged my kids to take a stance in their public school. Do not participate in that language and pray for discernment to make corrections when you hear it being used. In many cases, people are unaware of the magnitude of the power in their speech both positively and negatively.

While my kids take a stance in this area, it hasn't changed their friends' language all the time. They have however noticed that at least around them, their friends seem to try to avoid that phrase much more than they used to. Those friends have now replaced their language with alternatives like "oh my goodness" or "oh my gosh" and I consider this a great step in the right direction! It is encouraging to see the change my kids can have in their circle of influence—not simply with friends adjusting their speech, but the gateway it opens to even more conversations.

False Oaths

Another way we can sin against the Second Commandment is through false oaths. An oath engages the Lord's name. He is truth. Therefore we must respect His name in all matters of truth. False oaths include perjury and human speech. In the Sermon on the Mount, Jesus reminds us,

> "Again you have heard that it was said to your ancestors, 'Do not take a false oath, but make good to the Lord all that you vow.' But I say to you, do not swear at all;* not by heaven, for it is God's throne; nor by the earth, for it is his footstool; nor by Jerusalem, for it is the city of the great King. Do not swear by your head, for you cannot make a single hair white or black. Let your 'Yes' mean 'Yes,' and your 'No' mean 'No.' Anything more is from the evil one" (Matthew 5:7).

As Fr. Mike Schmitz explains, "Taking an oath or swearing is to take God as witness to what one affirms. It is to invoke the Divine truthfulness as a pledge of one's own truthfulness."[18] This is why it is

18 https://www.youtube.com/watch?v=Xt1HEvpoDyM

incredibly important to honor truthfulness when you make an oath. Your oath claims that God vouches for you and your declaration. If it is a false oath, you attempt to make a liar out of God for your own purposes. The assertion that God is contrary to what He is—truth—is what makes a false oath such a grave sin.

Another aspect of this Commandment is the importance of keeping the promises we make to God. When we make a promise to God it is proper to have the full intention to follow through on our promise. Again, God is truth. Therefore when we engage with God, He takes us at our word, and He gives us His word as truth.

My encouragement is to discern with great care when we make promises to God. I tend to be abundantly careful in this regard, as I know my limitations and weaknesses. I am much more inclined to ask God for his guidance and help along the way rather than declare my promise. I appreciate Thomas Merton praying,

> My Lord God I have no idea where I am going. I do not see the road ahead of me and I cannot know for certain where it will end nor do I really know myself. And the fact that I think I'm following your will does not mean that I'm actually doing so. But I believe that the desire to please you does in fact please you.[19]

This disposition allows us to bring our needs and desires to the Lord without the temptation to make promises we cannot keep.

To close out this section, I love the encouragement in CCC 2158-2159:

> God calls each one by name. Everyone's name is sacred. The name is the icon of the person. It demands respect as a sign of the dignity of the one who bears it. The name one receives is a name for eternity. In the kingdom, the mysterious and unique character of each person marked with God's name will shine forth in splendor ...

Everything the Lord asks of us, He also desires for us. He has called each one of us by name, in love and dignity. What a gift to live and act in a place of mutual respect and honor.

19 https://www.youtube.com/watch?v=vqtvB0_MqEM

Reflection Questions

Take some time to reflect upon the questions below. Consider writing in your Reconciliation journal or notebook of your choice. Invite the Lord to be present with you as you consider these questions.

- *What thoughts or feelings surfaced when reading this chapter?*
- *Did anything stand out to you as new or different than you had previously considered?*
- *Did the Lord convict your heart in a particular way?*
- *Are you moved to repent?*
- *Did you receive any interior movement in your heart, a consolation, or a deeper love for God or neighbor?*
- *What do you want to ask the Lord for now?*

Examination of Conscience - Second Commandment

Now that we have explored the Second Commandment, perhaps in greater detail than you have before, I invite you to sit with the Lord and review the following questions. What is He saying to you? Come Holy Spirit Come!

1. *Have I used the name of the Lord casually without due reverence?*
2. *Have I blasphemed God's name—through words of hatred, reproach or defiance?*
3. *Have I used language against God's name, Jesus Christ, the Virgin Mary, Christ's Church, the Saints, or sacred things?*
4. *Have I used God's name to curse other people?*
5. *Have I used God's name as an exclamation when I'm angry or surprised?*
6. *Have I unfaithfully made promises in God's name?*
7. *Have I made a false oath—swearing to take God as a witness to what one affirms?*
8. *Have I committed perjury—making a promise under oath with no intention of keeping it?*
9. *Have I used obscene language?*
10. *Have I respected God's name, my name and the name of others, respecting the dignity of persons?*

CHAPTER THREE

The Third Commandment—Keep Holy the Lord's Day

The Third Commandment is the conclusion of the Commandments that focus on love of God. Before we move on, I want to thank you and encourage you to keep on reading. The Lord has so much in store for you!

Our culture has changed in numerous ways from the accounts we recall in the earliest of centuries. God designed Creation for us to uncover and explore. Humanity certainly has made many medical, technological, and agricultural advances through its exploration. However, in parallel with some of these advances has also come the forgetfulness of the importance of our human dignity and connectedness to each other.

Spending time in rest, gathering in gratitude and "wasting time" building stronger relationships with God and one another is God's display of love to us. St. Teresa of Avila writes, "mental prayer is nothing else than a close sharing between friends; it means taking time frequently to be alone with Him who we know loves us."[20]

---

20 The Book of Her Life, ch. 8, par. 5.

Fr. Wayne Sattler reflects, "We certainly would not consider it wasted time for a mother to spend all day with her often sleeping infant. That frequent time spent alone enables a mother to come to know that little person in a way others will not."[21] We deepen and strengthen our relationships with God and each other when we set aside time to simply "be" with one another.

This is the beautiful "why" behind the command to keep the Lord's Day holy. God is not a jealous, prideful God, who demands we remember Him for His ego-sake. He is a loving Father who knows humanity so well that He places guardrails and guidelines for us. He does this so we can fully accept, receive, and grow into the wonderful people He created us to be. He knows that society and even we ourselves will place enormous pressure on us to "Do it all! Create! Work hard! Succeed! Never stop! Keep pressing!" While all these sentiments aren't evil in themselves, the Lord knows that we also need to rest. Rest allows us to appreciate the hard work we have achieved, to build relationships, and to have time to allow Him to refresh us. His greatest gift is the invitation to come and spend time with us as He nourishes us with the Eucharist.

Read CCC 2169.

We are reminded of Israel's liberation from the bondage in Egypt. We are reminded through our Baptism that we are no longer slaves. I invite you to feel the love of the Father and His loving concern for you as you read CCC 2172:

> God's action is the model for human action. If God "rested and was refreshed" on the seventh day, man too ought to "rest" and should let others, especially the poor, "be refreshed." The sabbath brings everyday work to a halt and provides a respite. It is a day of protest against the servitude of work and the worship of money.

What an awesome gift and reminder for us. God knows us. He knows we rush and race. He knows that we need to rest and be refreshed. He

21 *Catholic Exchange* article https://catholicexchange.com/wasting-time-with-god/

knows this life is hard and filled with many demands and tribulations. God loves us and provides for us. He provides His compassionate understanding for those of us who are charged like the Energizer bunny. For those of us who are so easily tempted to keep on going—distorting our true human capabilities and limits— as a loving Father, He gives us some tough love and requires us to stop and rest.

Sunday Obligation

Have you ever considered this reality of Mass: after a long week of work, He invites us all (His entire family of humanity) into His house (church), where He speaks His love and fidelity to us (Liturgy of the Word), feeds us His very self (Eucharist), blesses us (Final Blessing), and sends us forth from the Mass (Final Dismissal) to proclaim His Gospel of love as we go back into the world the following week. What an absolute gift!

I know the term Sunday obligation is used, but obligation sounds a lot like begrudgingly forcing. My heart instead wants to burst out in song and declare, "if this is an obligation, sign me up for overtime too!" How can Sunday Mass be called an obligation when it is literally the Father's answer to my heart's longing?

Whether you were raised in a loving home or suffered immensely in a dysfunctional home, today anew, the Father invites you into His home to care for you.

This is what that looks like for me: Every Sunday at Mass, God the Father scoops me up after a week of intense hard work—suffering, giving of myself, pouring myself into my family, coworkers, and friends. He tells me through timeless words and songs how much He loves me and how He continues to provide for me. He fortifies me with His strength and love. He provides His very self: body, blood, soul and divinity for me to consume and be nourished with His supernatural strength. He prays blessing over me and sends me off with an encouraging word to go out, with all the gifts He's given me, to transform the world in His name. He does the exact same thing for each one of us.

I don't know about you, but it makes me reflect on how much we all long to be loved and nourished in such a passionate and consistent manner. Sadly, more often than not, this is not what we experience in our families. Many childhoods are wrought with pain, neglect, and longing to be fully known. I invite you, if you haven't considered this perspective about what the Holy Mass is, that you set this book down for a moment and consider that God has beckoned you and wants to offer you what you may not have experienced in your family.

He is your loving Father offering you this sacred place to provide you everything that may lack. He wants to give you what your earthly family perhaps could or would not. It has taken me much time, prayer, and vulnerability to experience this. It has taken a combination of knowledge and faith, intellect and will, feelings, and unwavering truth to come to this realization.

Even on days that I don't feel anything, I can relish in thanksgiving for our Almighty God. I am so grateful that I have the ability to not only participate in Mass on Sundays, but that I get the opportunity to receive this miraculous gift every day at Daily Mass. I pray you too can respond to the great invitation you are commanded to receive as well. This command is disguised in some ways as the ultimate and essential gift given to you to actualize all the other Commandments.

The next time you hear the phrase "holy day of obligation," I hope you hear not a begrudging requirement, but rather the Father's invitation for you into extra special celebrations at His house. I hope you are filled with excitement and a sense of belonging that you've been invited to celebrate these most Holy and important moments in His and our lives with the Creator of the world!

Let us not only receive this great gift for ourselves but participate in Mass every Sunday with an expectant joy that compels everyone else around us to want it for themselves as well! If you have never experienced the joy of Mass in this way, then I invite you to ask the Lord to give you this gift. Give Him permission to mold your heart, to convert the areas of your heart that need healing, and pour His grace upon you. I imagine this prayer request would delight Him!

I love the final section in the *Catechism* about Sundays as a day of grace and rest from work. Read CCC 2184 and 2185 now. To summarize, we must rest from work on Sundays.

In the Bible, the Pharisees tried to entrap Jesus when He was healing on the Sabbath or when Jesus and the disciples walked through the field and ate the heads of the grain. Jesus reminded them, and us, that the Sabbath was made for man, not man for the Sabbath (Mark 2:27). The Sabbath was intended as a blessing and benefit for humanity. God offers it to us as a time of rest, physical refreshment, and spiritual renewal.

A Day of Rest

We are called to stop and smell the roses. We are called to work hard but also rest and enjoy the fruits of our labor. We are called to remember God and give Him thanks for our very lives and work. We are called to set aside time for our families to not rush off to multiple sporting events or activities but to truly be present to one another. We are called to enjoy the leisure time to soak in all the wonderful gifts we've been given.

Also, believe it or not, we are even called to soak in those terribly difficult seasons of life, so that we may appreciate ALL that He has given to us. Perhaps you or a loved one is currently experiencing a profoundly difficult season of life. You or your loved one may be battling a debilitating or terminal illness, the loss of a loved one, or some other great trial. The Sabbath is a time set aside for you to rest in His loving arms. He invites you to lay down your defenses, anxieties, and fears to let Him embrace, nourish, and minister to you.

Just like the other Commandments—we have to make a choice between what God asks of us and what we determine is best. The temptation to choose not to work or do house chores, grocery shopping, and the other necessities of life on Sundays is a real one. It takes a firm commitment and planning ahead to honor this Commandment. God is a good Father and knows what we need before we even ask (Matthew 6:8). Trust that if you honor this Commandment, He will make a way for everything to get done.

God gives us Sundays to rest, to keep it holy, to visit Him in His home where He longs to speak words of life over us, feed us, empower us, and send us forth each week renewed and refreshed to accomplish the mission He has entrusted us with.

Reflection Questions

Take some time to reflect upon the questions below. Consider writing in your Reconciliation journal or notebook of your choice. Invite the Lord to be present with you as you consider these questions.

- *What thoughts or feelings surfaced when reading this chapter?*
- *Did anything stand out to you as new or different than you had previously considered?*
- *Did the Lord convict your heart in a particular way?*
- *Are you moved to repent?*
- *Did you receive any interior movement in your heart, a consolation, or a deeper love for God or neighbor?*
- *What do you want to ask the Lord for now?*

Examination of Conscience—Third Commandment

Now that we have explored the Third Commandment, perhaps in greater detail than you have before, I invite you to sit with the Lord and review the following questions. What is He saying to you? Come Holy Spirit Come!

1. *Have I honored God, especially on Sundays and holy days of obligation?*
2. *Have I deliberately, without just cause, missed Sunday Mass?*
3. *Have I shown proper reverence and awe at Mass in my appearance and behavior?*
4. *Do I intentionally allow Sunday to be a day of rest and not a catch-up day to finish all the unfinished work of the week?*
5. *Have I engaged in commerce on Sundays making unnecessary demands on others that would hinder them from observing the Lord's Day?*

CHAPTER FOUR

The Fourth Commandment—Honor Your Father and Your Mother

As we enter into a discussion about the Fourth Commandment, we also shift our attention from love of God to love of neighbor. The remainder of the Commandments focus and instruct us how to love each other well.

I recall one brisk October morning driving home from an extended retreat filled with love, inspiration, and gratitude for all the ways the Lord had blessed me. I came home full of zeal and ready to share my enthusiastic joy with my family. As I pulled up in the driveway, my senses sounded the alarm. I opened the front door and to my panic, days old clothes were strewn across the house, limp fabric arms and legs straddled the walls and chairs. Socks to warm countless feet were cast in every direction with their abandoned pair partner nowhere to be found. One kid ran to hug me and almost knocked me over. Two more yelled at each other about the other coming into their room unannounced, and the refrigerator was ransacked. My husband's expression was one of stress and shell-shock of enduring the last few days. I was completely deflated. Love of the Lord just got real!

God showed me that His love is manifested in acutely tangible ways through our families. He demonstrated to me that love is a decision and an action. He gave me the silent retreat as a gift. Those times of silence and solitude with the Lord are crucial. They are when He infuses His love into us. He pours His love into us in the silence so that we can then pour out that love to others, first and foremost within our families. Love in families is like a mix-master highway with twists, turns, underpasses, overpasses, and endless construction barricades. Love is worked out in action, mistakes, forgiveness, mercy, and compassion. Read how CCC 2207 beautifully describes family and what we gain as a society when it functions within its intended design.

Scripture also illustrates the importance of family life aimed at building a strong domestic church. Ephesians 6:1-4 prescribes the family relationship:

> "Children, obey your parents [in the Lord] for this is right. 'Honor your father and mother.' This is the First Commandment with a promise, 'that it may go well with you and that you may have a long life on earth.' Fathers, do not provoke your children to anger, but bring them up with the training and instruction of the Lord."

The connection is that honoring and obeying parents is a foundational principle of how to live a God-honoring life. Furthermore, it is the responsibility of parents to train and love their children as God does.

Read CCC 2197-2200. They offer the foundation of the Fourth Commandment. Additionally, these paragraphs lay the groundwork for understanding how to love our neighbor in all subsequent Commandments.

The Family in God's Plan

Because this Commandment lays the foundation to which the other six follow, we need to spend time exploring all the elements of this

Commandment. So let's get to it. We begin with the section titled "The family in God's plan." Please open your *Catechism* and read paragraphs 2201-2203.

The family is the place where we have responsibilities, rights, and duties to teach and demonstrate God's love to our children. The Fourth Commandment came into sharp focus the moment my husband and I found out we were pregnant with our first child. While in many ways we were still relatively spiritually immature, we both innately sensed the great responsibility beyond ourselves that is required to bring children into this world. God pierced our awareness that a new landscape of love was on the horizon.

As God always does, He anticipated our needs and provided loving guidance and instruction for how to accomplish this mission. In prayer I heard the words of what became our parental mission statement. "Our job as parents is to show you that God loves you, that we love you, and you are to go out and share that love with others." This great commission of love is not simply a feeling; it is decidedly an action. As their first and best teachers, we are responsible to explain, express, demonstrate, and train our children on their way to salvation. Proverbs 22:6 states, "Train the young in the way they should go; even when old, they will not swerve from it."

One small display of God's sense of humor and delight in our humanity came through an exchange with my now teenage daughter. He witnessed to me that as He delights in our growth, we too can delight in our children's growth. God also confirmed to me that He has our back. There are so many uncertainties that come with rearing children. Sometimes we need reassurance that we are on the right path.

One day my daughter and I went to Confession together. Normally the lines are relatively short, however on this particular day they were the longest I had ever seen them. We exhausted our time in preparation for Confession and simultaneously looked at each other as if to say, "what do we do now?" The Lord always provides! I felt prompted to invite her to read paragraph 2217 from the *Catechism*. Take a moment and read it now.

As she read it, her faint smile grew more pronounced as she declared, "I don't like that." She looked at me with a dazzling smile on her face and a twinkle in her eye. Even as a young teenager she recognizes the beauty of truth; even when it demands much.

The gift of the *Catechism*, as an authoritative source of God's word and instruction, gives parents confidence and strength to lean into. God has our back! It's not my opinion on how children ought to behave. The Church helps us teach our children what their responsibilities are. It also teaches parents what our responsibilities to our children are. These declarations are rooted in God's truth, out of love for the good of us all. I am so thankful I don't have to invent it! On those days when I am worn out with yet one more decision to make, I thank God for His loving instruction and guidance.

It is worth noting that God gave the Fourth Commandment with a full understanding of how families are like the mix-master highways. Most families carry some amount of dysfunction and pain. However, He gives us His promise and His insights that if we are open to submit our wills to His leadership and wisdom, great things can happen!

My mom unfortunately was reared in an awfully difficult household. While certainly there were good memories along the way, a majority of her childhood was overshadowed with an alcoholic dad and volatile environment. Even as a young girl she found refuge in a nearby church. She shared with me a vision she had of herself in a crowd of other children, yet she was the one chosen to sit in Jesus' lap where He comforted her in the darkest of times. She would recall that moment of feeling wrapped in the Father's love throughout her life.

As she entered adulthood, she brought God's love into her marriage and sought to bring it to us as children differently than she experienced in her childhood. My mom submitted her will to God's and sought to follow His will to the best of her ability. All of my siblings love the

Lord immensely. That is a testament of how the Lord truly provides a guiding light. He offers His grace to redeem our wounds, allowing the future to look different than the past.

The opening paragraphs of this Commandment provided the foundation for all subsequent Commandments on how we are to love our neighbor. Imagine a world where your parents cherished, protected, taught and spoke life-giving words over you every day as you grew up. Imagine a world where your children obeyed out of love and duty, eager to appreciate your gift and sacrifices of parenthood! Imagine a world where your in-laws and parents of adult children knew their proper role and responsibility and lived out that encouragement and benevolence towards you and your future family. Imagine the schools where teachers lovingly pour their hearts into teaching your children the art of loving how to learn. Imagine these students respecting their authority; and viewing teachers not as adversaries, but rather treasured coaches assisting in the work the parents foster at home. Imagine a society that designs its policies to strengthen the family structure fostering the ability for families to thrive.

This is what the Fourth Commandment's wisdom offers us. Is it a tall order? Yes! Will we fall and make mistakes? Yes! Do we have the power through our Baptism and the Holy Spirit to get up and try again? Yes! An invitation to you here: I don't know what your upbringing was like. I don't know what your current family situation is. And I don't know the dynamics currently at play in your family. But, at this moment, will you consider asking the Lord to begin today to embrace His vision for family life and give you the motivation, grace, and perseverance to follow His command?

Each day we are given the opportunity to take one small step in the right direction. I think of all the times our kids (and we as parents) disobey, fail, and make mistakes. The tendency is to react with anger, embarrassment, or fear. I try to intentionally ask the Lord for help during these times. I ask Him to help me remember that my child's identity is as a beloved son or daughter of God; their mistakes don't define them. I ask God for the humility and wisdom to assist me in lovingly showing my children why we had the rule in place and how that rule is designed to help them flourish in virtue and love. With God's grace, employing this patient teaching approach with my children has been incredibly fruitful. Consequences are still issued but it is with loving understanding, a conversation, and a step towards conversion.

I won't sugar-coat this either. It truly takes God's grace to have the discipline to parent in this way. It is so much easier in the moment to yell, scream, or punish. Yet, this is not how the Lord has instructed us to operate. He has given us His guidance and the power of the Holy Spirit to follow Him.

Responsibilities of Children

Again I am impressed with the wisdom of the Church in the *Catechism*. It begins with the children's responsibilities to parents and authority. If I were asked to write a catechism, my instincts would be to begin with the parent's responsibility to their children. The Lord aptly reminded me through Isaiah 55:9:

> For as the heavens are higher than the earth, so are my ways higher than your ways, my thoughts higher than your thoughts. Yet just as from the heavens the rain and snow come down and do not return there till they have watered the earth, making it fertile and fruitful, giving seed to the one who sows and bread to the one who eats, so shall my word be that goes forth from my mouth; It shall not return to me empty, but shall do what pleases me, achieving the end for which I sent it.

Why does the *Catechism* begin with children's responsibility? Simply put, each one of us is a child, born to a mother and father, and if baptized, is an adopted son or daughter of God. Some of us may never become parents, or have siblings, but we are all children. God is always so good! Read CCC 2214 and 2215 now.

God is always first. His divine Fatherhood is what allows for our creation in the first place. He then gives that authority to our parents. Our parents, despite all the failings they may have, have given us the gift of our human life, and thus we must offer them gratitude and respect.

The respect that is owed to our parents is shown by true docility and obedience. As CCC 2217 beautifully articulates, "As long as a child lives at home with his parents, the child is expected to obey his parents in all that they ask of him when it is for his good or that of the family. 'Children, obey your parents in everything, for this pleases the Lord.'"

There is a misconception out there that children dislike rules and boundaries. That may be true in cases where the rules are unjust, however, for the most part kids and adults alike appreciate knowing what the boundaries are. I remember a phrase my dad would always say. "No. And it's one of my favorite things to say to you." He said it with a smile on his face. We knew he was serious but we also knew he said it out of love for us. We always knew where the line was drawn. Of course we tested him, yet he always held fast to the boundary line convincing us of its goodness and security. It's funny the things that you begin to say once you become a parent. I have adopted that phrase with a smile on my face and my kids truly know in our house, no means no, and I'm not afraid to use it. It breeds trust and security in our home.

Recall what you read in CCC 2217. Children are expected to obey their parents and those to whom their parents have entrusted them, in everything. There is one caveat: children need not obey instructions that are morally wrong, which sadly can happen.

I often have this conversation with my children. We talk about obedience in our home. It helps create order, good will, and smooth functioning in an extremely chaotic world. I try to remind them that the obedience we require is not out of pride (although sometimes we too fail and that does occur), but rather out of a desire to teach them how to listen to the Lord.

God is invisible, we are visible. How can they possibly ever learn how to obey an invisible God? They learn through the parent's visible demonstration of love and accountability. It is our job as parents to give our children the opportunity, training, and discipline required to practice obedience. It seems cruel to raise our children without a requirement of obedience—for when we turn them loose in adulthood, they would go out like sheep to the slaughter.

It is imperative that parents say what they mean and mean what they say. The Sermon on the Mount reminds us "let your 'Yes' mean 'Yes,' and your 'No' mean 'No'"(Matthew 5:37). Rules not enforced are a dangerous breeding ground for distrust. A lack of consequence, natural or other, breeds distrust. It suggests that the rule I laid down was hollow, unimportant, and unnecessary.

It is the same for our God and the Commandments! God gives us the Commandments because they are good for our flourishing. There are also consequences, natural or other, when we break the Commandments. This sorrow for sin, pain, and hardship that we experience when we sin against the Commandments demonstrates God's trustworthiness. It demonstrates that He had a purpose for the rule and He stands by it.

The objections children have when they don't want to obey almost always boils down to their will versus what has been asked of them. Isn't that always our objection too? Our will versus the Father's will? How do we learn how to align our will with that of the Father's, which is always the actual pathway that leads to our greatest fulfillment and eternal happiness? Children's obedience to parents is the primary training ground to learn how to form and align our wills with the Father's for our ultimate good. It is a huge undertaking to establish this dynamic in our families. It requires a lot of effort from both children and parents to establish this family culture, but it is an effort worth pouring yourself into and it produces much fruit.

Responsibilities of Adult Children and Siblings

That leads us to the responsibilities at the time of emancipation. Emancipation simply means the time when kids grow up and leave home to start their own lives and families. CCC 2218 says, "The Fourth Commandment reminds grown children of their responsibilities toward their parents. As much as they can, they must give them material and moral support in old age and in times of illness, loneliness, or distress."

Many of my friends, as well as my own personal journey, are sandwiched between simultaneously caring for children at home and caring for aging parents. This was my lived experience with my mom while she endured her stage four cancer illness, and with my dad in the years after she passed. My mom's suffering in the last year of her life was immense. It however was one of the most joyous seasons of my life. By joyous I don't mean happy, I mean a time of deep, abiding joy that came from the knowledge that I participated in the sacred story of a beloved.

There are many real challenges when it comes to following this Commandment to honor aging parents. Oftentimes it includes making a multitude of difficult choices, decisions, and sacrifices. It requires juggling your own responsibilities with work, family, and other obligations in addition to coordinating, ensuring, and being present for your aging parents. Even if parents were not a shining example of parenthood, they did give us life. Our response therefore must be to respect their inherent dignity and care for them in their need.

The last section on children's responsibilities involves the sibling relationship. CCC 2219 states, "Filial respect promotes harmony in all of family life; it also concerns relationships between brothers and sisters..."With all humility and meekness, with patience, [support] one another in charity.'"

My husband and I also spend a lot of time and energy to promote and foster strong sibling relationships amongst our children. We often highlight to them how God placed them here for one another. They were given to each other not only for today, but also extended into the future when they each will either have families of their own, or be called to a vocation of religious or single life. No matter their vocation, they will appreciate and call on one another as they enter and experience their futures together. Opportunities afforded between siblings may be the best training ground to learn how to be humble, meek, patient, and supportive, day in and day out.

Responsibilities of Parents

Next is the section on parents' responsibilities to children. Again, the *Catechism* outdoes itself in its beautiful articulation of the role of parents and children towards each other. Read CCC 2221-2228 once or twice before we move on.

CCC 2221 reminds me why I am so grateful for the ability to stay home with my children for much of their lives. Many financial sacrifices were made to enable this. To my amazement and sadness, in my nearly 20 years of parenthood I have encountered many parents who don't fully understand the absolutely incredible and important role they have as parents. So many parents give up their authority as the first and best teachers. So many do this because they've bought into the lie that they aren't able or qualified for the job. The Lord specifically designed each child for their particular family. I've made a ton of mistakes in my parenting career, but the one thing I can say without fail is that I have fiercely loved my children.

It's important to define love once again: "willing the good of the other." I have taken my God given call and responsibility to heart. I have sought to educate myself first, and then at least try to make a valiant effort in my children's moral education and spiritual formation. Furthermore, as we discuss society's role in the next section, it is my prayer that we, as a society, better value the importance of the role parents have, and create policies to support this great endeavor and responsibility.

CCC 2222 instructs us as parents to respect our children. Parents must remember that their children are gifts from God. They are given to us for a time as distinct, precious, and unique persons who by their very existence are worthy of dignity and respect. Parents must be committed to their own personal responsibility of obedience and relationship with God and then extend that knowledge, wisdom, and experience to their children.

CCC 2223 reminds parents of their responsibilities to their children. This paragraph especially contains so many treasures and expectations that need to be prayerfully considered. Do we as parents create an environment for our families where tenderness, forgiveness, respect, fidelity, and disinterested service are the rule? Does our focus promote these essentials or are we so consumed by other things: our work, our finances, our children's academics, sports, or fine arts programs that we have no time or patience to foster the essential elements of family life?

How many times have I failed? Too many to count, I assure you. But by the grace of God I am willing to go to my husband and children and admit my failures. I ask not only for forgiveness but for their prayers and encouragement to stay focused on the priorities that really matter. The world wants to distract us with the lure of many good substitutes, but we are called to recognize when those good things fall short of the best things.

At a youth group kick off event I was asked to present to the student's parents. My teenage daughter encouraged me to stress the absolute importance for the parents to foster their own real and authentic faith life. Even as a teenager, she sees that authentic examples and witness from parents in the home is the greatest evangelization tool.

So often parents foster a hollow example to check the box: go to church, youth group, or service projects without a real desire for a relationship. For some, the intention is not an authentic relationship with the Lord, but rather external vanity to look a certain way to the outside world. Kids are smart. They can see right through these charades. Hypocrisy to kids is like blood to a shark: they can sense it a million miles away. We owe it to our children to be intentional about our faith life and then create an environment where it can authentically grow and blossom.

It is important to pause here and reflect. If you are a parent, how do you describe your faith life? How do your kids describe your faith life? If you allow yourself to honestly and authentically assess yourself, the Lord honors your vulnerability. He will not condemn you for falling short if that is the case. He will inspire you to lean in and allow Him to pour His grace and fire into your heart. It is His greatest desire and our ultimate call to holiness to be in a deep, intimate relationship with God.

CCC 2224 emphasizes the role and importance of family life. How we rear our children is aimed at teaching our children how to be an active, contributing member of the family. These lessons allow that to translate into their role and contribution to the larger society when they come of age.

We also need to create an environment in our households that is filled with virtue. In our home, we have chosen to limit exposure to certain music artists, television shows, movies, and video games that promote a culture contrary to our values. I felt so fortunate when a friend shared her perspective of how to navigate these situations with kids from her own upbringing.

She said her parents judiciously choose to watch or listen to questionable content together as a family and then have a legitimate conversation about the content. They asked their kids how the lyrics, story lines, etc. aligned with the Catholic faith...or not. Afterwards they'd ask them if they felt more inclined to choose self-sacrificial love or selfishness.

I absolutely loved this idea and we have incorporated it into our family culture. We spend a lot of time not only telling our kids what not to do, but helping them think through these choices in a controlled, mature, and loving environment. We want them to learn how to think critically about what they choose to be exposed to now and in the future.

CCC 2225 discusses evangelization in the home and CCC 2226 employs parents as the primary catechists for their children.

These two paragraphs are paramount. I've often asked parish leadership and priest friends if they had to focus on one small segment of the parish life, who would they choose and why. While many varying answers and justifications came out of those conversations, I'd have to say the overwhelming majority agreed on young adults. I agree with their wisdom. If young adults are well-formed as they begin their families, they have a greater probability to follow the guidance in CCC 2225-2226 to teach their children to know and love God.

Our excitement and enthusiasm for the faith is contagious. I have personally experienced the love and awe of a truly intimate relationship with the Lord. I can no more hide it from my family than talking about an elephant in the room. God is my absolute favorite person to talk about. My kids see the evidence of my early mornings spent in prayer. They see my dedication and love of daily Mass. I talk to them about how the Lord works in my life at work, with friends, and through difficult circumstances. I share with them exciting encounters and fascinating adventures the Lord manifests all around me.

I asked my youngest son how he knows that I love the Lord. He parroted my husband's response about the time I spend in prayer and frequenting Mass. He then added with a really honest and endearing comment, "you also know how to hold back your anger." How perceptive for a nine year old. It's true, the Lord has transformed me in so many ways. It's not that I don't get angry, but I now have custody over my passions...at least most of the time.

CCC 2227 discusses family environments in our growth in holiness. I love this paragraph too! My children have 100% contributed to my growth in holiness.

Sometimes I fail to show my children love. When I realize I have failed them, I take my hurts, tiredness, exhaustion or whatever has plagued me to the Lord and ask Him to teach, forgive, and renew me. He always answers these prayers and I share my repentance with my kids. I ask their forgiveness for the time when I was less than. We are all human. Recognizing and rectifying our failures openly with one another breeds love, trust, and good will.

CCC 2228 concludes this section of the Commandment with inspiring words and encouragement. I hope you have experienced the same gratitude and wonderment at the words and guidance of our God and His Church, for us both as children and as parents. God has created us out of love, for love, and given us the ways in which we can bring His love to fruition. Each of these lessons in family life, known as the domestic church, trains us for our life outside of the home walls into the church and society at large. The more we can foster these lessons and virtues in our homes, the more we can change the world, one relationship at a time.

Responsibilities to Society

The final section of the Fourth Commandment discusses how its precepts affect and govern society at large. Similar to how God has given authority to parents in the rearing of children, He also "enjoins us to honor all who for our good have received authority in society from God" (CCC 2234).

In the United States, we have a democracy, but certainly not everyone we have voted into office has upheld the standards that God has given us. Be that as it may, we are still required to respect the authority of the position and pray and work towards creating and maintaining policies that are in alignment with God's commands. CCC 2235 states, "no one can command or establish what is contrary to the dignity of persons and the natural law." We have to actively pursue learning and embrace this standard of dignity of persons and natural law so that as a society we can champion its cause.

Regarding duties of civil authorities, read CCC 2236 to understand the standard for how civil authorities are to act. Those in positions of civil authority must hold themselves to this standard.

CCC 2239 describes the duties of citizens. We have a responsibility to show respect for authority, while simultaneously voicing just criticism to policies that are contrary to God's commands in truth and charity.

I am impressed with the way the *Catechism* concludes the Fourth Commandment. Read CCC 2244-2246. If you are in a position of civil authority, I implore you to spend some time with these words in an honest evaluation of whether or not you are in alignment with God's commands. You may not have been mentored in this perspective, but now you are given an opportunity to change history by adopting this perspective into your work.

The Church has the distinct and grave responsibility to stand as a wise parent shaping the borders that will allow societies and every person to prosper in their human dignity. There is certainly a lot of noise that surrounds the concept of separation of church and state. The Church's stance is not to create policies but rather highlights the principles in which we are called to observe. This ensures every human person can receive their due dignity expressly given as God's beloved creature.

Reflection Questions

Take some time to reflect upon the questions below. Consider writing in your Reconciliation journal or notebook of your choice. Invite the Lord to be present with you as you consider these questions.

- *What thoughts or feelings surfaced when reading this chapter?*
- *Did anything stand out to you as new or different than you had previously considered?*
- *Did the Lord convict your heart in a particular way?*
- *Are you moved to repent?*
- *Did you receive any interior movement in your heart, a consolation, or a deeper love for God or neighbor?*
- *What do you want to ask the Lord for now?*

Examination of Conscience—Fourth Commandment

Now that we have explored the Fourth Commandment, perhaps in greater detail than you have before, I invite you to sit with the Lord and review the following questions. What is the Lord saying to you? Holy Spirit Come!

1. *Have I honored my father and my mother—have I been disrespectful or disobedient to my parents?*
2. *Do I cause my parents unnecessary worry or trouble?*
3. *Have I given my parents respect, gratitude, just obedience, and assistance?*
4. *Do I treat my siblings with respect, love, and forgiveness?*
5. *Have I been lazy in my responsibilities?*
6. *Do I consistently work with civil authority for the building up of society in a spirit of truth, justice, solidarity, and freedom?*
7. *Have I been harsh, angry or oppressive in my demands?*
8. *Do I show respect and obedience to those who have authority over me?*
9. *As a parent, have I taken up an intentional pursuit of learning and witnessing my faith to my children?*
10. *As a parent, have I taught my children the Catholic faith and ensured opportunities to live a Sacramental life?*
11. *As a parent, have I neglected my children's physical, emotional, or spiritual health?*
12. *As a civil authority, have I given ample time for religious duties and instruction?*
13. *As a civil authority, have I imposed unreasonable policies?*
14. *As a civil authority, have I respected the fundamental rights of the human person by caring for the physical health and wellbeing of those under my care?*

CHAPTER FIVE

The Fifth Commandment—You Shall Not Kill

The *Catechism* opens this section by quoting Scripture: "You shall not kill. You have heard it said to the men of old, 'You shall not kill; and whoever kills shall be liable to judgment.' But I say to you that every one who is angry with his brother shall be liable to judgment" (Matthew 5:21).

This Commandment begins by establishing the founding principal and absolute importance of human dignity. CCC 2258 states:

> "Human life is sacred because from its beginning it involves the creative action of God and it remains forever in a special relationship with the Creator, who is its sole end. God alone is the Lord of life from its beginning until its end: no one can under any circumstance claim for himself the right directly to destroy an innocent human being."

This concept is so important for us to sit and pray with.

You, and every human being are important and sacred to the Lord. There are many scripture verses for you to read as God's love letter to you. Jeremiah 1:5, "Before I formed you in the womb I knew you, before you were born I dedicated you, a prophet to the nations I appointed you." Isaiah 49:15-16, "Can a mother forget her infant, be without tenderness for the child of her womb? Even should she forget, I will never forget you. See, upon the palms of my hands I have engraved you; your walls are ever before me." Jeremiah 31:3 "With age-old love I have loved you; so I have kept my mercy toward you." Every creature that has ever existed, and with special affection, humans, the Lord God has created out of love. He loves each one of us more than we'll ever be able to conceive.

Envision a time when you felt the most loved and the most seen from another human. That is merely a shadow of the magnificent love the Lord has for each one of us. This is the absolute truth and foundation that the Fifth Commandment is borne from.

Read CCC 2261 and 2262. The Church teaches and gives us guidance in the areas of legitimate defense, intentional homicide, unintentional killing, and war. I invite you to explore and expose yourself to her motherly guidance. God loves us so much and wants us to live!

As a society we have become desensitized to death through technology, video games, movies, and a culture that in some ways glorifies death. Ironically, despite all the areas we may desensitize ourselves to death, I've seen all too often the reality within our families that death is a topic of conversation that is avoided at all costs.

I hope this chapter is helpful to realize all of the ways death affects us and the precise reason the Lord calls us to champion those efforts to live our lives abundantly and fully. CCC 2262 reminds us of Jesus' words in the Sermon on the Mount and the high call He invites us to emulate.

Self-Defense and Punishment

Jesus always shows us the way through His word and example. All four Gospels account for when Jesus was betrayed and arrested. Peter knew it was an injustice for people to hunt down Jesus. Jesus was innocent of the crimes He was accused of. Peter was filled with righteous anger, and we too have probably encountered this more than once in our lives. However, Jesus showed us that inflicting violence out of anger; even righteous anger, is not His way. Not only did Jesus rebuke Peter for lashing out in anger, He went a step further and healed the man's ear (Luke 22:51).

Whenever we are tempted to lash out in anger, we can recall Jesus' passion. Jesus' scourging, beating, and ultimate torture was met with prayer, non-violence, and forgiveness. He did this to put sin to death. "He himself bore our sins in his body upon the cross, so that, free from sin, we might live for righteousness" (1 Peter 2:24). He ultimately brought about fruitful justice.

CCC 2263 on legitimate defense helps form our logic to assess situations that are gray. In no way does God ever allow for injustices without justice. But His thoughtfulness gives us inspiration and examples. This allows for our military, police officers, and even civilians to preserve life even if unintentionally they end another. Yet it is also a grave responsibility that we carefully and prudently form our conscience to not be deceived, for the evil one's greatest weapon is pride and confusion. We must be well formed in God's law so in the height of emotion, strife, and passion we act according to our disciplined virtue and not be swayed into sin and vice.

It is also helpful to keep the principle at the end of CCC 2266 in mind: "Punishment then, in addition to defending public order and protecting people's safety, has a medicinal purpose: as far as possible, it must contribute to the correction of the guilty party."

All of our actions to correct injustices are viewed with this lens—medicinal. When I relate this to how I parent, all corrections and discipline for my kids should be medicinal as well. Often in the throws of parenting, there is the temptation to punish out of anger and pride instead of true righteous correction. My husband and I discuss our parenting styles often and this concept is usually a part of the discussion. We are responsible to teach our children and correct their wrongdoings; otherwise how will our kids ever learn and grow? We must strive to discipline with prudence and love.

Hebrews 12:11 reminds us "At the time, all discipline seems a cause not for joy but for pain, yet later it brings the peaceful fruit of righteousness to those who are trained by it." Also, Proverbs is filled with wisdom about discipline. Proverbs 3:11-12 states, "The discipline of the Lord, my son, do not spurn; do not disdain his reproof; For whom the Lord loves he reproves, as a father, the son he favors."

This informs how the Church views the death penalty today. Historically there were inadequate means to keep persons that were a danger to themselves and others out of harms' way. With the penal system we now have in place in America, we have the ability to preserve the dignity of persons even after the commission of serious crimes. We can protect citizens, yet also not deprive the guilty the possibility of redemption. My friend, who I'll reference as David, has worked in the prison ministry for many years. He shared this story with me and it serves as a beautiful example of redemption and conversion.

When he was first asked to volunteer in prison ministry, David was extremely hesitant and scared. Afterall, he had a family to protect and provide for, and he was concerned at times for his safety. Within the walls of the maximum security prisons, there were more than a few men who had given up any sense of human dignity towards themselves and others. This absence of empathy and respect for life creates a dangerous environment for prisoners, prison staff, and volunteers alike.

David knew these potential risks. In prayer and assurance from the Lord, he took a leap of faith and forged on. He was one of the only volunteers who spoke Spanish and that gave him the ability to make small talk and jokes with some of the men who were a little more open. As he began to have conversations with some of the men, he noticed that they began to look at him in a different way. David shared profoundly relatable stories about how he lived through many of his own rough encounters in his early childhood.

These stories were relevant and resonated with many of these men, creating a sense of connection and trust. Eventually, those conversations turned into curiosity. They asked him questions about how he was able to avoid prison. They recognized that even though they were faced with extremely similar situations and circumstances, they found themselves on the inside of the prison walls, and David managed to stay out, in freedom. Through David's humility and compassionate conversations, he was able to "see" the men and help restore the hope and dignity that the prison walls had since silenced.

During his time in the prison yard, David noticed a smaller guy who was always off by himself in the corner. David and this man occasionally locked eyes with one another from a distance. One afternoon, David sensed the time had come to introduce himself. Surprisingly, the guy was the first to talk when David approached him. "Leo" proceeded to tell my friend that after weeks of watching him engage with the prisoners, he was so struck by his calm demeanor and level of comfort in such a terrible place. Leo asked David how he wasn't scared. Afterall, many of the guys only survive prison by projecting a menacing and intimidating posture.

David spoke of his trust in God and shared some of the relatable stories he had shared with the others previously. Leo and David developed a friendship. Through their conversations Leo shared that he had received the death penalty for his crimes. Leo acknowledged his crimes probably warranted the punishment he was given. Yet through these encounters with David, Leo decided he wanted to live out his remaining days in repentance, surrender, and atonement for what he had done.

Over several months, what started as a simple conversation ended in the conversion of this man's heart. David, again, through his humility and deep trust in God, was able to share the love the Lord has for all His sons and daughters despite the sins committed. What a beautiful gift and grace when repentance flows from receiving this deep abiding love. David's willingness to sacrifice and trust in God enabled him to journey and help restore another man's heart.

Leo eventually received the Sacrament of Reconciliation from a priest. While the laws in Texas ultimately ended this man's life, I can't help but think he was one of the living examples of why the Church promotes the protection for the sanctity of life from conception to natural death.

Abortion

It's now time to delve into some hot-button topics regarding intentional killing, specifically abortion. *Come, Holy Spirit, and open our hearts to receive your love. Penetrate our hearts and the brokenness within so that we can, with open hearts and minds, hear your love for us.*

There is a caveat before we tackle these challenging topics that is incredibly important to state. As so often happens with sin, there's usually not only one big sin that occurs out of the blue. There are many influences, decisions, and injustices that have likely occurred that led us to make certain decisions and choices. All of God's Commandments are intertwined with each other. For example, when we break the First Commandment to love and worship God and God alone, that may lead us to commit a sin against the Sixth Commandment by committing adultery. The effect of that sin, in conjunction with fear and other responses, may tempt us to commit a sin against this Fifth Commandment.

King David illustrates this concept of how sin layers itself. His choice to murder was precipitated by other choices. He made several smaller choices before ever coming to the decision to murder. In 2 Samuel 11 we are reminded that King David was supposed to be on the battlefield with his men. Instead, he stayed back in Jerusalem and we hear of his sins of lust for Bathsheba and then adultery. As the story unfolds, those sins led to more sins: lying, plotting, and ultimately the murder of Bathsheba's husband, who was also one of King David's most honorable men.

A similar scenario can be said for many cases of abortion. If I speculate for a moment, I wonder if many occurrences or opportunities to entertain the idea of abortion as an option can be led back to injustices and woundedness in a woman's life that eventually lead to this choice. That being said, to maintain the integrity of addressing each Commandment purely, we will discuss abortion in a straight forward manner. Then we will tackle the scenarios and choices that potentially lead to abortion in the chapters to come.

The Church teaching is very clear in CCC 2270-2272. I invite you to read those paragraphs now. The consequences of excommunication outlined in CCC 2272 can be a difficult pill to swallow, yet it is a necessary cautionary rule to help us recognize the severity this issue demands.

As stated at the beginning of this chapter, the Church establishes its principles on the foundation of the primacy of the dignity of life. Many pro-choice arguments stem from the debate of a person's secondary rights. The Church instead focuses on the primacy of protecting life so every person can have a life with which to base secondary rights. Our society has gotten caught up in arguments regarding secondary rights. It articulates the whys and reasons, yet loses sight that the Church's stance to give every person their deserved dignity is because God has willed their existence.

The right to life is the foundation upon which other laws can be made. If we do not take up our call and noble mission to safeguard life, we quickly see other secondary laws crumble, as well as societies at large. This is why the Church affirms the magnitude and gravity for all involved in the sin of abortion. The penalty issued by the Church is so severe because it is meant to communicate how important and fundamental this is to the dignity of persons and society at large.

We are reminded of the call for all punishments to be medicinal. There is such a strong response to the sin of abortion because it is such a serious and foundational offense against the dignity of human life owed to every person.

A lot of people may be unfamiliar with what excommunication is and the severity of the offense of abortion. The crime of abortion is so grave because it is literally stamping out the lifeblood of humanity. If we decide who is worthy or unworthy of life based on our preferences, we have taken a journey on a devastating road. We don't have to look far back in our own history books to see the devastating effects when humans decide who is worthy of life and those who are not.

Take a few moments and think of a handful of people who you treasure. People that at some point have loved you, cared for you, and made you feel incredibly cherished. Take this moment to thank God for them. Now, I'm willing to bet, they have also fallen short in some way to show you love. Imagine if someone decided, when this person was in their weakest, most broken state, that they were not worthy of life and killed this beloved person in your life. Who has the right to make that determination? Not me, and not you.

That is why we must fight to protect life from conception to natural death. We are all treasures; some broken, battered, and bruised, but all called beloved sons and daughters made in the image and likeness of God. We must do our part to ensure all the lives that God has willed to exist have the dignity to shine their light into the darkness.

Euthanasia

This leads us to the topic of euthanasia. CCC 2276-2277 clearly articulates how and why euthanasia is morally unacceptable.

This concept of euthanasia had a direct impact on me. Some of the most painful but beautiful moments in my life occurred during my mom's year-long final battle with cancer.

The night I received word of my mom's terminal diagnosis, I had an astonishingly powerful supernatural experience. My dad called me from the hospital room and told me that the doctors ordered a PET scan for my mom. In their words, "on the PET scan her cancer lit up like a Christmas tree." My mom's breast cancer from 18 years prior had metastasized and spread all over her body. It was everywhere; in her breast, lungs, lymphs, bones, liver...you name it, the cancer had made its home. The Lord spoke to me words I will never forget, "Carrie, I am going to give you the grace to be exceedingly present in every moment of this journey, but I am also going to give you a grace to see me display my glory during this time." I heard the Lord as words spoken in my own voice, originating from outside of me, but felt deep within my heart and mind.

For the purpose of this section, I share one day of her journey. It was the moment we all sat in the oncologist's office, a month or so before her passing when my mom decided to stop all medical treatments.

There was such a heaviness in the room. A tornado of destructive lies swirled around the room. One such lie was the sentiment that the world tries to sell us: quality of life trumps dignity of life. It was the lie that only vibrant lives are worth living. It leaves no room for God to work through the pain and suffering to manifest spiritual, mental, emotional, or physical healing.

I watched the pain in my mom's eyes and felt her life and joy wither under the weight of this ideology. So many fears of being a burden to her family: the treatments, medications, doctors visits, logistics, sickness, sadness, uncertainties...the list of toil goes on. She had carried the burden of feeling invisible for a large majority of her life and in some ways I sensed her resignation to the lies of the evil one that she wasn't worth the effort. In my eyes, nothing was further from the truth.

Late that afternoon, mom and I sat at the kitchen table alone together. I asked her point blank about her decision. This is when she shared so many stories of her upbringing, of her struggles, of her insecurities... all raw, real, and vulnerable. I remember tears streaming down my face and the Lord brought to mind the image of Aaron and Hur holding up Moses' hands—one on one side, one on the other—so that Moses' hands remained steady till sunset (Exodus 17:12).

I told my mom, I'd be her Aaron and Hur; if she wanted to continue to receive treatments, I would go to every length needed. The love that passed between my mom and me in that moment is one that cannot be described in words; only in groanings too deep for words. The sacredness of two people fully embracing God's truth together in unity against the lies of this world is incredibly powerful.

There is more to this life than what our physical senses can perceive. The invisible workings of God are ever present in every moment, despite what our senses may suggest to us. Spiritual healing manifested in my mom with the telling of every story that she had previously hidden within her heart. Now she had a sacred listener on the other end to receive her heart fully in love.

Physical healing is always temporary, but what we cannot see is the healing work in the heart that occurs even if we can't perceive it physically. That is why the Church implores us to respect life from conception to natural death. Euthanasia would have taken away those spiritually powerful and healing moments. I am so thankful that my mom was offered the opportunity to experience all of those invisible yet powerful and healing moments with God.

Read CCC 2278. The Church in no way suggests one treatment philosophy over another. Rather, she demands that we love each human person and never put an end to the lives of the handicapped, sick, or the dying. We must leave that to God's Providence.

CCC 2280 continues to communicate this important truth, that "Everyone is responsible for his life before God who has given it to him. It is God who remains the sovereign Master of life. We are obliged to accept life gratefully and preserve it for His honor and the salvation of our souls. We are stewards, not owners, of the life God has entrusted to us. It is not ours to dispose of."

Suicide

Everyone who has been affected by suicide knows the great pain and remorse felt by a life cut short. Not too long ago I attended a funeral of a high school friend who committed suicide. I left in such sadness. I thought how everyone spoke of so much love for him and yet somehow that love was not absorbed into his heart. Or perhaps he felt love, yet was still desperate to escape his emotional pain or feelings of worthlessness.

Thoughts swirled in my mind: where did we fail to show him that love, or speak God's truth to him about his inherent dignity and worth? Lord, in what ways do I currently fail to show those around me what a gift they are, not because of anything they do or don't do, but solely because of who they are? Do I take the time to notice suicidal thoughts or tendencies in others and offer an appropriate outlet to help talk them through it?

It caused me to consider and evaluate if I take every opportunity I have to love like God loves us and speak those words of love to those around me. Like King David, so many choices and decisions are made before this tragic life-ending choice (2 Samuel 11:1-27). It speaks to why we all must continue to grow in the spiritual life. We must inform our consciences and grow in holiness, virtue, and love of God, ourselves, and our neighbor. We are our brothers' and sisters' keepers and we must take these opportunities to receive God's love and pour out that love to them.

Scandal

We now discuss the sin of scandal. This is a category of sin that most of us likely are unaware of, never allowing it to rise to our consciousness. I can think of several examples of ways I have unknowingly committed this sin. Once I became aware of its devastating effects, I had to wrestle under its weight. In honesty, I have lamented how difficult and what sacrifice it takes to avoid being ensnared in the traps of scandal.

CCC 2284 does a great job defining scandal: "Scandal is an attitude or behavior which leads another to do evil. The person who gives scandal becomes his neighbor's tempter. He damages virtue and integrity; he may even draw his brother into spiritual death. Scandal is a grave offense if by deed or omission another is deliberately led into a grave offense."

Think about every conversation you have in a day. When you lament or gossip at work or school, does it cause the other person to think it's ok to talk in this manner? Potential scandal. When you are silent in a room of people spewing untruths, mistruths, or lies about another, has someone that respects your opinion deemed those lies as truths now because of your silence? Potential scandal.

I've had several debates with friends about a particular book and movie series because of the potential scandal it creates. I am still undecided on whether or not the books and movies are evil. However, because I do think there is potential for their content to promote evil, I err on the side of caution. I do not want to contribute to the damage of virtue and integrity within my household. Therefore we disallow those particular series to avoid scandal.

My husband and I are our children's protectors and guiding lights. We must take that responsibility seriously. Therefore, our limits of certain media aren't borne out of close-mindedness, but rather prudence. If one of my children felt strongly that they'd like to read or watch the series, we discuss the content. We embark on a discovery journey together. We'd engage in truly open discussions about real effects of exposure that particular content might have on them. Together we'd commit to pay attention to and watch for behaviors, choices, and actions after reading and watching that media to see if the inclination to sin, disobey, gossip, or grow in anxiety were heightened and then adjust accordingly. We are our brothers' keepers. We must always be vigilant that we do not cause another to sin because of our action or inaction.

The sin of scandal can also be in the language that we use. I've had to correct my older children to amend their language at times because little eyes and ears are always watching. It is a reality that the younger ones make decisions to choose vice or virtue by the older one's example. It is an incredibly high standard, yes, but also one that when viewed with the proper disposition, helps protect the innocent and allows us to grow in virtue and love together.

I love the stern yet important warning issued in CCC 2287. It is reminiscent of Jesus' warning in Matthew 18:6-7, "Whoever causes one of these little ones who believe in me to sin, it would be better for him to have a great millstone hung around his neck and to be drowned in the depths of the sea. Woe to the world because of things that cause sin! Such things must come, but woe to the one through whom they come!" We must take Jesus' and the Church's warnings to heart. We must be vigilant in all of our words, actions, and deeds to ensure we don't cause anyone to sin by our example.

Respect for the Body and Health

This instruction ties into the next topic which discusses our bodily health. CCC 2290-2291 discusses practices that for many are so ingrained in our everyday lives that we are not even aware of their sinfulness. Sometimes we don't even realize when we choose a lesser good without a second thought.

The Lord loves us all so much and thus shares His wisdom that each of these temptations can lead us down a dangerous path if used without prudence. Unfortunately, recently my middle school daughter and our entire community was affected by someone who sinned in this manner.

My daughter's schoolmate was training for her cross country team. One evening she ran one of the common trails while it was still light out. A man who later was confirmed as intoxicated, barreled down the 30 mph road at over 60 mph. He hit this sweet precious girl. It has been over nine months now and she still has a long road to recovery ahead of her. She and her family's life will never be the same.

The Lord is always at work, and it has been incredible to witness how the community has come together to support this family. Yet, I can't help but wonder what our lives would look like if we all did our part to work on our own healing to avoid these terrible situations. Imagine a world where all baptized persons pursued holiness and wholeness with intentionality and diligence. What would the world look like if we took our call to evangelize seriously and ministered to the broken and wounded?

Just like the devastating effects of alcohol abuse, the same can be said for the use of illicit and illegal drugs. Unfortunately again, I have seen drugs destroy the lives of many people in my life. There is a huge temptation to minimize the magnitude of drugs and their effects in general. However, as I've experienced with virtually every Commandment and teaching in the *Catechism*, there is so much wisdom offered and when heeded can truly be the activator to experience a fulfilled life. I am filled with compassion for those who turn to drugs to cope with the hardships and sufferings in this life. So often it appears to be the only option to minimize and dampen the hurts of this world. This is precisely why we need each other and Jesus to know He has so much more in store for us.

The Lord provides a respite and safe space for all of our afflictions. Sometimes we have to be courageous enough to share His love and compassion for those who don't yet know His abounding kindness and mercy. The more that we experience God's love and mercy in our lives, the more we grow in confidence to share Him with the people that we love.

More often than not, drug use starts out as a small experimentation or curiosity and builds over time. Sometimes it can be easily overcome, but, unfortunately, too often I've seen it consume its victim. There is no condemnation in those who have used or are currently using drugs. Rather, it is a loving invitation that the Lord has so much more for us. We need one another to encourage and support each other through our hardships and trials. We need to create space for each other's hurts and pains so we can more confidently trust in the Lord's goodness and help to do the necessary work to overcome these addictions.

Connected to the use of drugs is the broader category of drug trafficking. That is a problem that seems to be increasing in our time. This quest for money and dominance often achieved through drug trafficking has tumultuous effects. As mentioned in the *Catechism*, trafficking is scandalous and evil as it encourages practices gravely contrary to moral law.

Drugs are often directly associated with the sins we will cover in the next chapter. But also, the use and promotion of drugs oftentimes ends in death either by suicide or accidental overdose. I have personally been affected by family and friends who have overdosed on drugs and died as a result. The gaping hole that is felt by no longer having the ability to experience their laughter and the gift of their presence due to these sins is crushing. Any and all efforts to eliminate drug trafficking assists in combating these evils.

The Church values all of our lives and it helps us to form our conscience in regards to scientific research. CCC 2292 highlights the Church's understanding that "Scientific, medical, or psychological experiments on human individuals or groups can contribute to healing the sick and the advancement of public health." Experiments are licit as long as they are not in themselves "contrary to the dignity of persons and to the moral law." Experiments must maintain physical and psychological integrity proportionate to the help achieved and minimize avoidable risks. They must also have informed consent from the subject or those who legitimately speak for them. Organ transplants are in conformity with moral law with exception of any direct disabling mutilation or death of a human being.

CCC 2297 highlights the necessity for respect of bodily integrity. Most people agree these guidelines are sound in logic and not generally controversial.

I love the next two paragraphs in the *Catechism* as they illustrate God's loving attention and care for us in our final stages of our earthly life. Read CCC 2299 and 2300 now.

I've shared earlier about the great grace in being at my mom's bedside when she left this life for the next. She had been anointed by one of our dear priest friends in the weeks leading up to her death. The entire day of her death was filled with family and friends surrounding her bedside, singing praise music, and praying as each of us was inspired. One of the most profound experiences came as our dear friends, a deacon and his wife, brought Jesus in the Eucharist. In the moments right after she received the Eucharist, my mom turned non-responsive and began the active dying process. What a gift to be wrapped in prayer and music, which was her joy, and witness her last perceptible experience being fed by Jesus Himself as food for her final journey!

Peace and War

The final two sections in the Fifth Commandment are concerned with peace and avoiding war. The Church goes into great depth surrounding the issues of military, war, and civil authorities. I am so thankful for those men and women who serve our military and serve as first responders. They offer sacrifices that I can only begin to imagine. Since my personal experience is limited to graciously accepting the fruits of their efforts and not their lived experiences, I am deferring the nuances of how these special positions are handled to the *Catechism*.

CCC 2302 reminds us, "By recalling the Commandment, "You shall not kill," our Lord asked for peace of heart and denounced murderous anger and hatred as immoral." Deliberate hatred is contrary to charity. We are called to love our enemies and our neighbors. Earthly peace is the image and fruit of the peace of Christ. Jesus declared in the Sermon on the Mount, "Blessed are the peacemakers, for they will be called children of God (Matthew 5:9). CCC 2307 summarizes the Church's position about war.

CCC 2309 goes on to say, "The strict conditions for legitimate defense by military force require rigorous consideration." Many of my friends work for a defense contractor and constantly have to pray and assess their work under this high call of rigorous consideration. CCC 2327 summarizes its stance well when it states, "because of the evils and injustices that all war brings with it, we must do everything reasonably possible to avoid it. The Church prays: "From famine, pestilence, and war, O Lord, deliver us.'"

Reflection Questions

Take some time to reflect upon the questions below. Consider writing in your Reconciliation journal or notebook of your choice. Invite the Lord to be present with you as you consider these questions.

- *What thoughts or feelings surfaced when reading this chapter?*
- *Did anything stand out to you as new or different than you had previously considered?*
- *Did the Lord convict your heart in a particular way?*
- *Are you moved to repent?*
- *Did you receive any interior movement in your heart, a consolation, or a deeper love for God or neighbor?*
- *What do you want to ask the Lord for now?*

Examination of Conscience—Fifth Commandment

Now that we have explored the Fifth Commandment, perhaps in greater detail than you have before, I invite you to sit with the Lord and review the following questions. What is the Lord saying to you? Holy Spirit Come!

1. *Have I directly and intentionally murdered—through performing an abortion, having an abortion, aiding someone procuring an abortion, euthanasia, withholding ordinary means to a dying or terminally ill patient, suicide, attempts of suicide, or serious thoughts about committing suicide?*
2. *Have I engaged in any form of fighting, quarreling, unrighteous anger, hatred, or desires of revenge?*
3. *Have I engaged in gluttony—through excessive eating or drinking, drunkenness, abuse of alcohol, medicine or illicit and illegal drugs?*
4. *Have I endangered other people's lives or my own—through drinking and driving, driving too fast, daredevil stunts, carelessness in leaving out poisons, dangerous drugs, or weapons or given drink to others knowing they will abuse it?*

5. *Have I participated in the mutilation of the body—such as castration, vasectomy, tubal ligation, hysterectomy (without sufficient medical cause), or immoral scientific research and its applications?*

6. *Do I give injury to health—taking contraceptive pills which may or may not be abortifacient, use of prophylactic or barrier methods to avoid pregnancy, use licit means of avoiding conception while fostering a contraceptive mentality or direct sterilization?*

7. *Have I set a bad example or caused scandal by my actions or inaction?*

8. *Do I have respect for the dying or the dead—do I champion a philosophy of dignity of life instead of quality of life?*

9. *Do I show aversion or contempt for others—through refusing to speak to them when addressed, ignoring offers of reconciliation especially between relatives, cherishing an unforgiving spirit, ridicule, insults, irritating words and actions, sadness at another's prosperity, rejoicing over another's misfortune, envy at attention shown to others, tyrannical behavior or inducing others to sin by word or example?*

10. *Have I caused unnecessary suffering or death to animals?*

11. *Do I work for peace and the avoidance of war?*

CHAPTER SIX

The Sixth Commandment— You Shall Not Commit Adultery

I love this Commandment so much; mainly because it goes to the source of our identity as persons and plays out in almost every area of our life. If you read "you shall not commit adultery" and say to yourself "well, I'm not married," or "I've never cheated on my spouse, so this chapter doesn't apply to me," you may be surprised by what's in store.

The real gift of this Commandment is that it encompasses all aspects of our sexuality and any act against our sexuality. That affects us all—men, women, children, married, single, laity, and religious alike. There is so much to unpack in this Commandment. So while I may not cover everything as deeply as you might like, I pray you'll come back to the Commandment on your own in prayer. I pray you will spend some time looking at how it affects your life personally and how the Lord calls you specifically to greater understanding, obedience, and virtue.

The first four opening paragraphs of this Commandment in the *Catechism* are written so eloquently. I invite you to read CCC 2331-2334 before moving on.

CCC 2331 reminds us that we were made in God's own image with the capacity and responsibility of love and communion. We see this exemplified in Adam and Eve as well as in the mystery of the Holy Trinity. The simplest explanation of the Trinity that most resonates with me is the combination of two statements: God is Love, and the explanation of the Trinity expressed as the Lover, the Beloved, and the Love between them.

This resonates with me because I can clearly see how this explanation is also revealed in the Divine Order of marriage. God created man and woman, complementary in their sexuality to love, to be loved, and thus be fruitful and multiply as an expression of that love. We have been given the capacity to love intimately. Arising out of that intimate love is the gift of children to perpetuate God's kingdom.

Our bodies are so important, crafted and designed as part of God's loving Creation. From a biological standpoint, I was fascinated when I realized something that I always knew academically but had never considered the awesomeness of it as it is related to our identity and purpose as humans: God designed all of our bodily systems to function on their own except for the reproductive system.

Our circulatory system functions independently to circulate blood throughout our bodies. Our muscular and skeletal system provides form, support, stability, and movement to the body. Our hematopoietic or lymphatic system functions to provide blood production, maintenance of fluid balance, and defense against disease—and so on and so forth. Every one of these particularly complex systems is specifically designed and performs its function independently within our bodies.

However, only the unique reproductive system requires the complement of the opposite gender to complete its ultimate function and purpose. The reproductive system's primary purpose is to reproduce. It requires the integration of male and female to perform its veritable function and purpose of existence. This incredible fact about the uniqueness of this reproductive bodily function is worth pondering intently. I marvel at God's creativity! The design within our own bodies is the mark of the Creator. Why did God make this particular body function dependent when all other body systems function independently? The answer: His plan for humanity is built into our very bodies.

Because of the sacredness of this particular bodily system, you can bet it is the area the evil one is most prone to attack. We certainly see that throughout all of time, and I'm guessing you've also experienced it in your own life or in someone that is close to you.

The beauty of God's design of male and female humans is what sets us apart from the angels. God has given humans the ability to co-create life with Him. Thomas Aquinas in his *Summa Theologiae* states, "Consequently the first sin of the angel can be none other than pride. Yet, as a consequence, it was possible for envy also to be in them."[22] In this revelation the angels saw that a nature lower than them (humanity) was to be hypostatically united to the Person of God, the Son, and they would have to submit in adoration to the majesty of Jesus, the Incarnate Word.

Satan's pride would not submit to adore something viewed as inferior to his own capability and nature. This pride was the primary reason Satan fell. In my own contemplation of these scholarly accounts, I surmise that it would not be a far stretch of rational thought to think that God also revealed to the angels of His plan to create man and give us this reproductive ability. This is a unique gift that He had not given the angels. Due to the combination of God giving humans a power He didn't extend to angels, as well as asking the angels to serve lowly humans, Satan's pride reared its ugly head and he and a third of the angels would not submit to their own limitations.

22 https://www.newadvent.org/summa/1063.htm

If you remember, this echoes the topics covered in previous Commandments about our requirement to accept that God is God, the Creator, and everything else—including humans and angels—are creatures subject to various limitations. Is it any wonder why Satan would then choose to attack and distort the very source of His sin? Satan is the father of lies. John 8:44 states, "He was a murderer from the beginning and does not stand in truth, because there is no truth in him. When he tells a lie he speaks in character, because he is a liar and the father of lies."

Temptation and Shame

Satan uses an unfortunately effective tactic—he lies to us and suggests, via temptation, that the sin we are considering is no big deal—until we commit it, and then he is the first to accuse us that we are beyond God's mercy and should be full of shame. Fulton Sheen is credited for saying, "Before the sin, Satan assures us that it is of no consequence; after the sin, he persuades us that it is unforgivable."[23] Shame is a powerful emotion that keeps most of us living in darkness—especially as it relates to the Sixth Commandment.

The battle most of us experience is when we fall victim to Satan's temptations. The problem arises when we distort this great gift of capacity and responsibility to love as God loves. Humanity often fails to love as God loves, especially regarding our sexuality whenever we use each other, lust after, or dominate one another. We are made to be gifts of self love but because of our concupiscence as well as the supernatural perpetual attack on this particular gift from God, we find so much brokenness especially in this area of our lives.

Genesis 3:9-24 paints a picture of the existential human experience. To summarize the scene: Adam and Eve sin, they blame each other, they hide from God, God questions them to open a dialogue about their actions, God curses the serpent, God offers pains of childbirth and work as toil as a remedy and cause to love sacrificially, clothes

23 https://www.azquotes.com/quote/1025976#google_vignette

Adam and Eve, and banishes them from the Garden as a protection from eating from the Tree of Life, thereby saving them from eternal damnation.

Reflecting on the scene, and considering our own lives, is it any wonder when our first parents sinned, they too hid from God? But what is God's response? Genesis 3:9 tells us, "The Lord God then called to the man and asked him: Where are you?" Obviously it's more of a rhetorical question as God knew where they were. The Scripture verses go through a litany of questions God asks Adam and Eve. These questions display God's desire for a relationship with them as well as His desire to help them explore the root cause of their disobedience. God does the same for us today. When we feel convicted about a sin, God does so not to condemn us, but rather to help us better understand ourselves. He shows us how and why we chose a lesser good than what His Will offers us.

God is full of justice and mercy. The justice He issues is to not vengefully punish. Logically we can quickly come to the conclusion that if God was only interested in punishment for punishment's sake, He wouldn't have taken the actions He does throughout the scene. Discipline and justice is a necessary good.

When we continue reading Genesis, we see that after issuing justice, God cared for Adam and Eve and clothed them. Just as for Adam and Eve, God is concerned with our eternal salvation and ramifications that are now in place due to our choices. God banishes them from Eden not as a punishment, but as a loving safeguard to protect them from further harm and eternal separation. God set up added protection for Adam and Eve to ensure their safety by placing angels to stand guard for them lest they be tempted again.

We too are given a guardian angel to help us in times of temptation. CCC 336 states, "From its beginning until death, human life is surrounded by their watchful care and intercession. 'Beside each believer stands an angel as protector and shepherd leading him to life.' Already here on earth the Christian life shares by faith in the blessed company of angels and men united in God."

Like with Adam and Eve, God is always pursuing a loving and intimate relationship with us. When we sin—and we will—He wants us to come to Him to help us understand why we chose a lesser love. He wants to rectify, forgive, and teach us. God does not shame us, He loves us and wants to bring us closer. He invites and shows us how to more closely resemble His image and likeness that He created us in.

Recall the many stories within the Bible, including the woman at the well (John 4:4-30), the woman caught in adultery (John 8:1-11), and the healing of the invalid by the Pool of Bethesda (John 5:1-18). Each of these encounters Jesus calls to mind the sin but never shames them. In fact all of these characters of their own accord go out glorifying Jesus' goodness and the miracles He performed, both spiritual and physical. The Holy Spirit will convict us of our sin for the express purpose to heal and transform us. Satan's only goal is to shame us after sin, while simultaneously tempting us into the next one.

The greatest power we have is to allow Christ to shine His light on these darkened places exposing Satan and his temptations for what they are. God knows us intimately and has given us His Fatherly instruction to fulfill our deepest longings and ultimate happiness. This chapter strives to provide transparent examples, so you can know you aren't alone. We all fight similar struggles and battles even though the specifics may look different.

I pray that you enter this chapter with me with a docile and open heart to the Lord. I pray you will dare to step outside of yourself and your way of thinking for a moment and ask Him how He wants to speak into your heart about this Commandment. He loves us all so much. This Commandment is a revelation of God's heart of love towards us. He is a powerful protector who gives us the required tools to not live a life full of shame and selfishness—not to control or limit us, but to give us freedom and protection!

Chastity

As we dive into the particular ways we sin against this Commandment, it was helpful to me personally to understand the Church's teaching on chastity from a broader perspective. I realized for much of my life I had an elementary understanding of what chastity is and why it's so crucial to understand.

The Church's teaching on chastity is helpful in framing our understanding of the Sixth Commandment more clearly. When we have a proper understanding of the beauty and power of chastity, it has the ability to discipline our minds, hearts, and bodies to fully embrace this Commandment, as well as better understand the ways we sin against it. CCC 2337 defines chastity so please take a moment to read it a couple of times.

In all honesty, I had to sit with this paragraph for a while to really let it sink in. I had to break it down in smaller pieces to understand what it was trying to communicate. What does the phrase "successful integration of sexuality with the person" mean? And next, what does "inner unity of man in his bodily and spiritual being" mean?

We are physical as well as spiritual beings. Our sexuality is an important aspect of our physical being. Different from animals, we are also spiritual beings who possess passions, intellect, and will. When those three aspects work in harmony, one can say there is inner unity of man in his bodily and spiritual being. The fullest expression of human love involves the sexual integration of the reproductive bodily system in males and females to produce new life out of that gift of self to one another. In the lived experience, this is when each spouse truly sees their partner as a beautiful treasure. Each knows that treasure carries with them a unique personality, gifts, longings, and desires. They each willingly choose to sacrifice all they can to offer themselves as a gift. They speak and give life emotionally, spiritually, and physically to their beloved.

When we have a clear understanding of, and have rightly ordered our desires physically, emotionally, and spiritually as it relates to our sexuality, we have total unity within ourselves. When we understand with our logic the proper design and use of our sexuality, bring that knowledge into our hearts, and discipline our will to act out of this truth, we experience a peace that comes with having everything aligned. It's kind of like when you hit that baseball right in the sweet spot—everything absolutely feels right. Most baseball players say that the way they KNOW they've hit a home run is when they feel no vibration at all. The same is true when we allow chastity to guide us: everything interiorly is aligned.

CCC 2338 summarizes this point beautifully.

> **2338** The chaste person maintains the integrity of the powers of life and love placed in him. This integrity ensures the unity of the person; it is opposed to any behavior that would impair it. It tolerates neither a double life nor duplicity in speech.

God has given us the incredible power of love and responsibility. This is extremely hard work and requires vigilance to be sure, but the freedom and peace we receive when we pursue this truth is unparalleled. In other areas of our life, we have experienced glimpses of what God offers us when we choose a disciplined effort towards chastity.

Endless hours of batting practice results in hitting the ball on the bat in the sweet spot. Singers achieve harmony among voices in an *a cappella* piece of music as a result of hours of rehearsal and perfecting specific vocal techniques. Artists study colors and shading techniques to result in the masterly crafted artwork. Dancers tirelessly commit their bodies to stretching and training to create the straight beautiful lines. Each of these examples require great effort and discipline to achieve the beauty they intend to communicate. So too is true with chastity.

Fr. Mike Schmitz offers that "chastity is 'a school of the gift of the person.'"[24] When we master ourselves, it enables us to offer ourselves as a gift to another. Here is where chastity bears fruit in the form of true friendship. God calls everyone to this virtue, no matter his vocation.

CCC 2339 discusses how we progress in chastity. It begins by stating, "Chastity includes an apprenticeship in self-mastery which is a training in human freedom. The alternative is clear: either man governs his passions and finds peace, or he lets himself be dominated by them and becomes unhappy."

Continue reading the entire paragraph as it gives us the head knowledge of what to do. As GI Joe stated in the popular 1980s animated series, "knowing is half the battle." Then the hard part and the real work begins. We have to take what we know to do and utilize the tools that have been given to bring our minds, hearts, and wills into alignment.

In his book *Mere Christianity*, C.S. Lewis writes,

> Chastity is the most unpopular of the Christian virtues. There is no getting away from it; the Christian rule is, 'Either marriage, with complete faithfulness to your partner, or else total abstinence.' Now this is so difficult and so contrary to our instincts, that obviously either Christianity is wrong or our sexual instinct, as it now is, has gone wrong. One or the other. Of course, being a Christian, I think it is the instinct which has gone wrong ... God knows our situation; He will not judge us as if we had no difficulties to overcome. What matters is the sincerity and perseverance of our will to overcome them. Before we can be cured we must want to be cured. Those who really wish for help will get it; but for many modern people even the wish is difficult ... We may, indeed, be sure that perfect chastity—like perfect charity—will not be attained by any merely human efforts. You must ask for God's help. Even when you have done so, it may seem to you for a long time that no help, or less help than you need, is being given. Never mind. After each failure, ask forgiveness, pick yourself up and try again. Very often what God first helps

24 https://www.youtube.com/watch?v=5N6aWCK_NIA

> us towards is not the virtue itself but just this power of always trying again. For however important chastity (or courage, or truthfulness, or any other virtue) may be, this process trains us in habits of the soul which are more important still. It cures our illusions about ourselves and teaches us to depend on God. We learn, on the one hand, that we cannot trust ourselves even in our best moments, and, on the other, that we need not despair even in our worst, for our failures are forgiven. The only fatal thing is to sit down content with anything less than perfection.[25]

Pray to Grow in Virtue

The greatest tool we have is prayer. Many years ago in a particularly difficult season of married life, I remember praying diligently for elements in my marriage to change. I knew there were aspects that were contrary to how God designed us to live in our married vocation. After about six months of intentional daily prayer, as well as many conversations with trusted friends about my situation, I distinctly remember the day of change. I had reached the end of my rope.

I cried in despair on my living room couch. Every emotion poured out of my heart as I cried out to God in desperation. I finally talked to God truthfully and allowed Him to do the same. I showed Him my anger, hurts, and disappointments. I went line by line with God about everything I didn't understand about my marriage. For me it was why, despite all our apparent efforts, we couldn't achieve the emotional, spiritual, and physical intimacy that we intellectually knew was available for us in marriage.

What happened next will stay with me for the rest of my life. I heard God speak in my interior voice that I had some choices to make. He wrapped me in His love and consoled me in a way that no friend had been able to do. He spoke into my heart without words but with what I can only describe as a warm blanket around my heart that convicted me that He had heard my lament. In a way that only God can, He asked me questions like He did with Adam and Eve. He asked surprisingly practical questions

25 Lewis, C. S. *Mere Christianity*. William Collins, 2012

that led me down a path of thought I hadn't previously considered. He challenged me. He invited me to see the areas of strength I brought to the marriage and asked me to fully embrace those and with His help, use those gifts more fully. He invited me to repent in the ways that I had allowed my hurt to fester and become bitter and resentful in my heart, even if I didn't always show that to the outside world. He also invited me to repent of my areas of sin.

My marriage didn't miraculously change overnight...but I did. And so did my prayer life. I encountered the Lord in vulnerability and trust and He pulled me closer to Him. I realized I had been using my prayer as a weapon of sorts (dressed up in really pretty, convincing, and even some true arguments) instead of a conversation with my Creator.

I was in essence telling God to change all the things about my husband and our situation that I didn't like or understand. In that sometimes frustrating season of prayer, the Lord patiently showed me the purpose of prayer isn't always to get an answer (my will, my wants). It is rather to enter into a relationship with Him so He can show me how much He knows me and heal all the areas of brokenness and hurt. He wants to do all of these things for me. My choice is to be willing to respond to His invitation to trust Him with my whole heart. This was a game changer.

This experience of what I know as true, authentic prayer, allowed me to trust that God's word is *the* Word. As we struggle to overcome sin in general and more specifically within our relationships, true authentic prayer is the primary weapon we wield to crush our sins. Why? Because this allows Jesus in to fight the battle He has won for us.

Temperance

CCC 2341 reminds us of the value of developing the cardinal virtue of temperance in our efforts towards chastity. Temperance is a vital skill for our ability to discipline our passions. When we speak of the passions; they are gifts from God. The passions are explored in the

Catechism and I urge you to read these teachings independently. For our purposes we will focus on the below paragraphs.

> **1771** The term "passions" refers to the affections or the feelings. By his emotions man intuits the good and suspects evil.
>
> **1772** The principal passions are love and hatred, desire and fear, joy, sadness, and anger.
>
> **1773** In the passions, as movements of the sensitive appetite, there is neither moral good nor evil. But insofar as they engage reason and will, there is moral good or evil in them.
>
> **1774** Emotions and feelings can be taken up in the virtues or perverted by the vices.
>
> **1775** The perfection of the moral good consists in man's being moved to the good not only by his will but also by his "heart."

The Church teaches us that the passions are neither morally good nor evil in themselves. However, when we apply our reason and will, what we do with those emotions can be morally good or evil. Ephesians 4:26 gives us the most succinct advice about the passions, "Be angry but do not sin; do not let the sun go down on your anger, and give no opportunity to the devil."

Temperance assists us with permeating our passions—our emotions—with logic. Every day there are multiple opportunities to experience many varied passions and it is our responsibility to put them under submission to our intellect and will. This can be as common as if someone says something to me that instantly sparks anger. I have the responsibility out of love and charity to stop in that moment and pair logic with that emotion before I react. I must consider if there is any truth to their comment. I must seek clarification if necessary and extend charity to them if I know their actions arise out of fear or stress.

The same concept applies to our sexual passions. Most of us will experience intoxicating emotions towards someone we find attractive and are drawn to. That attraction in itself is neither morally good nor evil. However, the circumstances surrounding that experience requires us to use our reason and will to act rightly. If I am married and that attraction is directed and fulfilled in my spouse, then it is morally good and rightly ordered. If, however, I am married and direct those passions to someone other than my spouse, or if I am unmarried and I direct and fulfill those passions, it is morally disordered.

In this day and age, I compassionately understand the instinctual rejection of this, and clever justifications pop up like the old whack-a-mole carnival game. Why? Because all too often we are not experienced or disciplined in temperance. It is simply a reality that we as humans are disposed towards selfishness and want what we want; sometimes whether it is good for us or not. It is the spiritual battle to overcome these temptations. It takes real grit and humility to ask for the power of the Holy Spirit to give us the grace to do so. It is an actual reality that we cannot do on our own...nor does God ask or expect us to.

God acts through Church teaching to encourage us in loving compassion for our lived experience. The next few paragraphs speak to the real difficulty and challenge this Commandment requires.

> **2342** Self-mastery is a *long and exacting work*. One can never consider it acquired once and for all. It presupposes renewed effort at all stages of life. The effort required can be more intense in certain periods, such as when the personality is being formed during childhood and adolescence.
>
> **2343** Chastity has *laws of growth* which progress through stages marked by imperfection and too often by sin. "Man . . . day by day builds himself up through his many free decisions; and so he knows, loves, and accomplishes moral good by stages of growth."

The Church understands and sympathizes that we all grow in maturity and experience with each passing day. She knows that we will have frustrating seasons of life marked by imperfection and sin. That fact doesn't stop her, as our loving mother, to encourage us to rise to the honorable call we've been given. God the Father, Jesus our Savior, the Holy Spirit our Advocate and help, together with Mother Church, will never abandon us in their continual encouragement and guidance to help us strive for holiness and true authentic happiness.

Paragraphs 2344 and 2345 from the *Catechism* remind us that God is not a dictator who issues a near impossible task. He is a loving Father who knows the beauty and goodness in what He asks and the happiness we experience when we fully live this Commandment. He doesn't expect us to learn it overnight nor without any failures. He gives us tools, His power, and His encouragement to persevere in this long, exacting work.

I think it's also important to remember St. Augustine's experience that he shared for our collective good when he said, "Lust indulged became a habit, and habit unresisted became a necessity."[26] Jesus came to set us free from the bondage of slavery. We have all certainly felt what St. Paul describes in Romans 7:15, "What I do, I do not understand. For I do not do what I want, but I do what I hate."

With this compassion towards ourselves and others, let us enter into the conversation about the ways we can sin against the Sixth Commandment in the loving embrace of the Father that seeks to bring us to the highest good and fullest life in freedom.

Lust

> **2351** *Lust* is a disordered desire for or inordinate enjoyment of sexual pleasure. Sexual pleasure is morally disordered when sought for itself, isolated from its procreative and unitive purposes.

This definition that the *Catechism* gives us is fairly straightforward. Most of us have likely been tempted by lust. It is important to make a distinction here that the Church does not say that enjoyment of sexual pleasure is morally disordered. It is morally disordered when

26 https://www.catholicstoreroom.com/2017/01/04/habit-becomes-necessity/

this awesome gift is self-seeking in nature, sought for itself, misused, or isolated from its procreative and unitive purposes.

This is especially important when I talk with my teenage children who are of dating age. They are designed by God to naturally desire this attraction to a potential future spouse; it's important and a true gift, in proper time and order! However, prior to the bond of marriage (and even within marriage, as we will explore later), lust can be incredibly damaging to the relationship.

We have to be aware of how connected our spiritual, emotional, and physical senses are to one another. There is much to be said about the realities of the consequences of sin. Sometimes we forget or haven't given much thought to put two and two together. Sin will always cause a negative effect on us. Some may say that claim is over-spiritualizing. A quick thought exercise can illuminate this claim rather clearly.

I am involved in parish youth ministry and therefore have a lot of exposure to many stories of our young people learning how to navigate their lives. One particular girl comes to mind who shared her persistent anxiety. She was able to identify that it comes in waves. Through prayerful questions and reflection, she allowed herself to examine and attempt to track the pattern of when her anxieties peak. She realized that anxieties often spiked after she submitted to a sexual temptation. This is an extremely revealing observation and shared by many. It suggests not necessarily that all anxiety is bred from sin, but it suggests that sin produces some form of anxiety. For this reason, temperance is critical to protect ourselves and each other from devastating consequences.

Masturbation

As mentioned previously, sin has a proclivity to more sin. Lust is usually a precursor to the sin of masturbation. Read CCC 2352 now.

Masturbation is a huge topic that unfortunately in many ways is the elephant in the room. So many parents have no idea how to broach this topic with their children, especially in those delicate years that lead up to puberty and the all-important teenage years. So in most cases they simply don't. These missed opportunities can have huge ramifications for their children's present as well as future relationships.

The sexual urges and impulses we have are divinely created as gifts. Properly ordered, they are given to increase the love and unity between a married man and woman and have the power to literally co-create another human life out of that love. There is nothing more awesome than this reality. Each one of my children were created from a beautifully intentional and loving embrace with my husband. Though conception didn't occur with every encounter of intimacy, we were always open to the possibility. This is part of the Sacramentality of Marriage. The sexual union between married persons is the visible sign of an invisible reality. It is the tangible witness of the Lover, the Beloved, and the Love shared between them. It changes everything when we truly understand the magnitude, beauty, and power of marriage, and the essential role sex plays.

Men can be affected differently than women in this regard, though it is a pretty touchy subject for everyone. In order to offer a balanced approach for male and female readers, my husband shares his perspective and insights as well.

From my husband's perspective, the concept of when two become one flesh in Ephesians 5:28-31 is paramount. The translations of words can be slightly different, but fundamentally he desires that we cleave—we cling, we adhere, we abide together in every aspect and manner in our relationship. To cleave is the invisible sign of perfect unity. It's akin to sheltering in the foxhole of life together: sacrificing and struggling together as a unit.

When my husband is confident in my absolute loyalty, commitment, and desire to cling to him, he can heroically protect and provide for me and all of our children. Unwavering unity comes from the knowledge and confidence that he is respected and honored. Out of this desire for complete unity, his sexuality then becomes his expression to offer himself as a gift physically. His desire to visibly present this invisible reality of complete unity is accomplished through the physical gift of his sexuality.

The two ends of marriage are the good of the spouses themselves and the transmission of life. This literally means my husband's ability and my receptivity to his sexual expression is essential for our relationship and family to flourish. When we cleave to one another through the ups and downs of life our sexuality can be at times wonderfully recreational as well as deeply intimate, always rooted in deep respect and love for one another.

Denying this aspect of his masculine identity, fashioned and witnessed through his very body, can be psychologically, spiritually, and physically destructive. Equally destructive is a husband not loving and sacrificing for his wife. The price of intimacy is sacrifice. Sacrifice is caring for the other through a cancer diagnosis, an extended time of unemployment, or other physical, spiritual, and emotional crises. Borne from our inherent human dignity, we each deserve that kind of commitment. Our children deserve that kind of commitment. The life, death, and resurrection of Jesus is our authentic example of this commitment lived out. God desires this deeply intimate relationship with us and He paid that price of intimacy with His one and eternal sacrifice for His children.

Now we must enter into the dance. Our fallen nature creates the propensity to get this beautiful gift decidedly wrong. This area may be the greatest battle some have to fight, but fear not, God has given us His instruction and power of the Holy Spirit. Isaiah 41:10 reminds us, "Do not fear: I am with you; do not be anxious: I am your God. I will strengthen you, I will help you, I will uphold you with my victorious right hand."

For the seasons in life that I questioned my ability and readiness to receive more children into our lives, my husband was respectful of my fears of becoming pregnant. Instead of begrudgingly abstaining, he truly embraced me and my dignity as his wife and as a woman. He made the sacrifices to respect those times that we needed to abstain. Was it hard? Absolutely. He openly told me the difficulty and restraint it took to, in his words, "wake up next to a beautiful woman and have to resist his truly human instincts to want to engage in the sexual embrace." He however practiced the virtue of self-denial, temperance, and prudence out of love for me, his beloved wife.

This has far-reaching effects. I can tell you that all women know when they are being objectified. Now, it is true that there are many women who use this power as a weapon, and that is equally disordered. We have all felt what it is like to be used. Whether that is sexually, or even more generally, in friendships, in the workplace, at home etc. We'll dive into this more during the Seventh Commandment, but the reason I bring it up here is because when my husband chooses to deny himself out of love for me, that effect reverberates in every area of our relationship.

This carnal sacrifice carries over into acts of love, willing my good outside of the bedroom. He displays this love through his commitment to a sometimes frustrating or stressful job because it provides for us. He displays his love when even after a long day at work, he comes home and instead of distracting himself on his phone, he helps the kids with homework. Another display of his love in those early days of rearing our children was looking at me with the knowledge that I had reached my threshold. My day didn't need one more disruptive moment involving a whiny toddler. He lovingly would take over and allow me a few minutes to myself.

How on earth do these displays of sacrificial love relate to masturbation? Masturbation in itself is an intrinsically and gravely disordered action because it is entirely selfish and self-seeking. It removes the other person from the sexual act entirely. It no longer is a gift of self, but only self focused. It develops a demeanor of selfishness and 'taking care of oneself' at the expense of any and everyone else. It reflects your character.

Are you selfishly motivated? Do you put yourself before virtue and other people?

These are courageous questions to ask yourself. The abundant fruit and blessing of anyone, men and women alike, who are willing to accept the challenge to exclude masturbation from your life, will experience a freedom and a generosity that extends in ways well beyond their home. The denial of this particular sin creates a disposition of self-sacrificing love that Christ has called us to emulate.

I invite you to try, and see how working to eradicate this sin impacts your relationships. It won't only impact those relationships with those closest to you, but even those who are outside your inner circle. It will have a huge ramification and impact on those around you. They may never be able to tell you why something seems different about you, but they will notice the change.

All this awareness of sin is not to bring condemnation and judgment, but rather bring understanding of what God offers us in the alternative of these sins. We have to know what constitutes a sin and why it is a sin to be able to freely choose God's way over our own. God shows us that masturbation leads to a life of selfishness and self-absorption. When we deny our selfishness, we not only avoid sin, but we take a huge leap in growth and virtue that affects everyone around us more positively.

It is also important to include the Church's compassionate assurance: "To form an equitable judgment about the subjects' moral responsibility and to guide pastoral action, one must take into account the affective immaturity, force of acquired habit, conditions of anxiety or other psychological or social factors that lessen, if not even reduce to a minimum, moral culpability" (CCC 2352).

What does this mean? It means we are human. It also means God is a loving Father who instructs us in our ways within the bounds of our human limitations and natural growth. There is a lot of learning, disciplined effort, natural development of maturity, and growth required and gained over time.

Fornication

As we continue on, we come to the topic of fornication which I think is especially relevant to our young people. The *Catechism* defines fornication in CCC 2353 as a "carnal union between an unmarried man and an unmarried woman. It is gravely contrary to the dignity of persons and of human sexuality which is naturally ordered to the good of spouses and the generation and education of children. Moreover, it is a grave scandal when there is corruption of the young." Fornication includes any and all sexual acts between "first base" and "home."

This is an area that can be the most frustrating and tempting especially for unmarried couples when the physical attraction is very high. It is certainly a challenge for engaged couples who intend to marry but are still in the time period before marriage. This may seem like an impossible task to avoid fornication but surprisingly secular research supports this stance.

In the late 1990s my future husband and I took an undergraduate sociology class as an elective together.[27] The purpose of the class was to provide a sociological perspective on the institution of marriage and family structures. Any guess as to what this class, at a public state university, claimed as the number one cause of divorce? Cohabitation. Couples who live together before marriage don't survive. There are many factors at play here but when we train ourselves in self-denial for the good of the other, it has lasting implications. You may tire of hearing it said over and over again, but our determined noes give way to very powerful yeses in the future...it is worth it!

Pornography

Next we move on to a very prevalent issue that plagues our current society. In many ways pornography attempts to reshape the very foundation of human relationships. Read CCC 2354 to expand your understanding of the underpinnings of pornography that make it

27 https://catalog.tamu.edu/undergraduate/course-descriptions/soci/

so destructive. This sin is clearly defined as a grave offense in the *Catechism*. This clear declaration of gravity invites us to take special note of its entrapments.

Pornography has certainly proliferated since the advancement of technology. Gone are the days where you might find a magazine hidden away under a bed. With our phones and the internet, a plethora of pornography in varying degrees is available with a click of a button, along with its devastating effects. A friend permitted me to share a very personal story to offer hope and solidarity.

He was in college dating the girl of his dreams. They had been described as "good Catholics" because they went to Mass and outwardly seemed to be doing all the right things. However, as we've certainly all experienced, most of our sins are hidden in the darkness. He shared that one evening after she had fallen asleep at his place, he worked on his homework. He got bored and restless with his studies and eventually clicked onto some pornographic images. Some time had passed and his girlfriend awoke and saw him masturbating to these images. She watched silently and motionless for a few minutes collecting her thoughts. She felt so many emotions ranging from anger, to hurt, to insecurity, to doubt. All of these emotions compelled her to abruptly get up and storm out of the room, intent to never return.

He chased after her. Instinctually, she knew that this was a deal breaker for her and their relationship. When he caught up to her, she told him how much she loved him and how she also thought they could have a great future together. They were on the same page on so many levels, but this was an area that she was not willing to compromise. Either he gave her his full promise to never engage in pornography again or she needed to end the relationship.

He recounted that she said all of these things so calmly and with such conviction that he knew what he needed to do. In his mind's eye, he also saw the potential of their beautiful future together. He replayed all the moments that he watched her with young children, knowing she would be an amazing mother. He knew she was smart, loyal, and dedicated. All of those good things were worthy of the effort to make this promise to her.

Many years later, with a beautiful family and the wife of his dreams, he can say that he never engaged in pornography since he made that promise. There were other challenges to be sure, but he also confidently asserts that the discipline required was well worth the limited satisfaction he got in those empty moments of physical pleasure alone.

Before the temptation to despair takes hold, if his story seems impossible, take solace in knowing that there would not be the sheer number of books, studies, and resources available discussing pornography if this was not an issue that significantly affects a great number of people. My friend and his story is perhaps an outlier in his ability to quit pornography outright. He offered his story to give a reason for hope that it is possible to quit, without dismissing the real challenges of the grip of the addictive nature of pornography.

According to Addiction Center,

> Humans are susceptible to forming addictions to substances or behaviors that stimulate the brain's dopamine center, which causes intense feelings of pleasure. Like drugs, alcohol, video games, and sugar, pornography triggers a dopamine release in the brain. When someone has an orgasm, the body releases endorphins and there is a spike in dopamine levels, causing the person to experience feelings of pleasure similar to when someone uses drugs or alcohol. Dopamine is not the only chemical in the brain affected by pornography. Other chemicals affected by pornography include norepinephrine, oxytocin, vasopressin, endorphins, and serotonin. When activated by porn, the combination of these chemicals can cause issues, including shrinkage, cravings, and chemical bonding. Shrinking of the brain's frontal lobe can happen when someone abuses drugs, alcohol, or pornography. The frontal lobe is responsible for making rational decisions, so when this shrinkage occurs, so does a person's ability to make sound decisions.[28]

28 https://www.addictioncenter.com/behavioral-addictions/porn-addiction/why-is-porn-addictive/#:~:text=The%20Science%20Behind%20Porn%20Addiction&text=Humans%20are%20susceptible%20to%20forming,dopamine%20release%20in%20the%20brain.

There is a lot of information about pornography as it plagues so much of society. Recently I attended a presentation about human trafficking, a largely unspoken about pandemic of our time. It was asserted that pornography is the greatest root cause of human trafficking. Pornography shapes sexual desires, is used in the grooming process to desensitize victims, exploits victims, and alters our brain. It creates false expectations that ultimately hurt relationships.[29]

As our *Catechism* mentions above, we need to become educated and support one another in helping our brothers and sisters strive for freedom from this sin. These are very real challenges physically, emotionally, and spiritually to battle. St Nikon of Optina said, "You can only conquer a passion when you do not consider it as part of you."[30] All of these areas of sexual temptation and sin aren't part of you. Rather, they are vices separate from our identity as a person. God continually gives us the grace to overcome sin victoriously.

Prostitution and Rape

Closely linked to pornography is prostitution. Please read CCC 2355 as it descriptively illustrates why prostitution is so harmful to both the offender and the offended.

Prostitution does so much to destroy human dignity and relationships. At its foundation it creates an entire system of using and being used. The effects are far reaching to those directly involved and spreads its tentacles of darkness even to those not directly involved.

A dear friend of mine shared a story with me that left me speechless. She was married to an abusive and alcoholic man. Prior to their marriage, she was not aware of his many destructive tendencies nor their far-reaching effects. She was young with young children and had to learn how to navigate this destructive situation and relationship.

---

29 Bouche, 2015, *Fight The New Drug, The Truth About Porn*, Pace, 2014

30 https://orthodoxchurchquotes.wordpress.com/2014/09/12/st-nikon-of-optina-we-must-consider-all-evil-things-even-the-passions-which-war/

Soon into their marriage they settled into a familiar routine. He worked the second shift so he was never home for dinner or kids' bedtime routine. She became accustomed to his pattern of staying out into the early morning hours playing poker with friends after his second shift work ended. One evening he arrived home exceptionally late. He had been drinking but was not stumbling drunk. She figured he had played cards, lost money, and went searching for excitement elsewhere.

When he got in bed, she embraced him and initiated intimacy. He did not respond to her advances so she tried harder. The guilt hit him. In response he forcefully kicked her off the bed, entirely onto the floor, and told her he had been with a prostitute. She relayed to me that it was the most devastating thing she could have imagined and brought her to fetal position on the floor. My heart broke when she said, "I was not enough, and he said that in real words. A once confident woman turned into someone who no longer had any idea who she was."

I understand there are a lot of factors at play within this story, but it illustrates the demoralizing, dehumanizing actions, and lack of dignity offered to one of God's beautiful daughters. As the *Catechism* says, prostitution is a social scourge and we have to work to eradicate this sin. If you have partaken in prostitution, this is not a condemnation to you, but a wake-up call that God has called you, and those you love and love you, to so much more.

Closely linked to prostitution is rape. CCC 2356 expounds on the definition as well as the consequences of the sin. In my time spent leading women's studies, I have been shocked by how many women have been affected by rape. As more information comes out regarding human trafficking and even scandals within the church, I know many men who were also victims of rape in their youth.

Rape is especially abhorrent when committed against children. It has long lasting effects on their mental health well into adult life. Without proper help it can lead to extremely complex and dark realities. We must do our part to create strong domestic churches to protect our youth. We must again be ruthless in our attempts to weed out sin and work towards the greatest good God has created us for.

Homosexuality

The conversation now turns to chastity and homosexuality. As someone who has been deeply affected by this situation, I want to proceed with the utmost compassion. It requires such compassionate love and delicate handling.

I am brought back to the beginning of this chapter when we are reminded that our sexuality was potentially the very source of Satan's fall and thus humanity's subsequent fall. The evil one will use any method or tactic to thwart us from trusting in God's goodness and receiving His love; especially with regard to sexuality. I think each one of the three paragraphs in the *Catechism* dedicated to chastity and homosexuality sheds light on a very complex and currently controversial topic.

Read CCC 2357. I have many friends who are offended by the wording and sentiment of this paragraph, or at the very least, hurt and confused. However, in most cases when we take a moment and read it line by line with a trusting heart docile to God's loving instruction, perhaps it can be heard in a different light.

Some friends have said "the church calls me disordered for my sexual attractions." It is important to clarify this misconception. The Church timelessly declares we are all made in the image and likeness of God. In this specific paragraph, it states that homosexual acts, not the person, are intrinsically disordered.

Homosexual acts are disordered because the two primary purposes of sex are unity and procreation. Sexual complementarity is part of God's natural law. Homosexual acts do not allow your body to complete reproductively what it is designed to do. Homosexual acts go against the very purpose of their intention. This is why the Church uses the language it does.

I appreciated when Fr. Mike Schmitz said, "Sometimes we want things that are not good for us. God made you good but we're all broken. We all have concupiscence. We all have things that we desire that we have to say no to if we're going to actually become the people God wants us to be."[31]

We all have some area of disordered affections, perhaps not with sexual orientation. Anyone that says otherwise might be experiencing a blindspot.

Disordered affections can be any and everything from eating an unhealthy amount of chocolate cake to desiring wealth and fame at the expense of our family's emotional, spiritual, and physical needs. Simply because we have disordered affections, or passions, does not mean we have a right to engage in them. Actually, when we resist these passions in charity and love, the Lord brings about greater goods in our lives. God has a plan for all of our lives. Our brokenness, no matter the form, doesn't disqualify us.

With each difficulty arising from any of our desires not aligned with God's commands and truth, we are called to unite it to the sacrifice of the Lord's Cross. In the moment it feels like a burden or sacrifice, but over time, oftentimes in hindsight, we can truly see the beauty that occurs when we choose virtue over vice. I love CCC 2358 because it addresses many of my friends' experiences. I encourage you to read it especially if this is an area of familiarity.

The *Catechism* concludes this section with CCC 2359. Again she gives us her motherly wisdom, guidance, and encouragement.

I understand that I personally do not have to undergo this specific trial and some may say that disqualifies me to speak about this topic. However, I have a close middle-aged friend who has chosen chastity. She has resisted sexual activities despite her passions and opportunities to choose otherwise. The same can be said for my priest friends.

31 https://www.youtube.com/watch?v=sR0rIe4CPoA

Another friend shared with me how, for many years, he struggled with same sex attraction. He very vulnerably shared with me that he experienced much shame in some of the choices and behaviors he previously engaged in. He said over time the Lord truly redeemed him and showed him great mercy. He also relayed that he can honestly say he isn't consumed by the desires that he once was. Each of these friends have chosen obedience and docility to God's commands. They have worked to temper their desires to allow God to flourish in their lives.

Additionally, I appreciate some Catholic influencers[32] who have spoken publicly about their journey with this cross of same sex attraction. Their stories offer much hope and compassionate understanding to the many people who are burdened with these trials.

We all want to be loved in a very tangible and special way. We want to be somebody's "one." So for those who bear the cross of same sex attraction, there can be real pain in this trial. This exemplifies the need for a strong community to support one another. We are our brothers' keepers. Some crosses are heavy and we are called to love and support our brothers and sisters in all of our journeys to holiness.

Through true abiding friendships we can help and support each other. Philial love is a gift. By prayer and sacramental grace we all attempt to approach Christian perfection. Christian perfection is striving to become a saint. God has placed this desire for holiness in all our hearts and there are many obstacles along the way. All of our crosses, no matter what shape they take, can become the very ways and means to our sanctity if we allow them.

I have traveled this road with many friends. It has been a very difficult and hurtful road. There were times filled with misconceptions, a determined effort to combat lies from the evil one, and an absolutely committed heart to love—to will the good of another—no matter the cost. I pray for an outpouring of grace upon all that either personally

32 https://boldlybeloved.com/

have homosexual attractions or have close family and friends that have to bear this cross. We always remember that truth and charity can never be separated, and that willing the good of another is always achieved by following God's will and not our own. No matter what sufferings we must endure in the process, God will give us the grace we need to do His will if we ask and trust. *Lord, in your mercy please pour your grace into our hearts and fill us with your love.*

The Love of Husband and Wife

The next section of the *Catechism* discusses the love of husband and wife followed by conjugal fidelity. The first half of CCC 2361 states, "Sexuality, by means of which man and woman give themselves to one another through the acts which are proper and exclusive to spouses, is not something simply biological, but concerns the innermost being of the human person as such. It is realized in a truly human way only if it is an integral part of the love by which a man and woman commit themselves totally to one another until death." The second half of the paragraph illustrates this ideal as it recalls Tobias and Sarah's prayer in Tobit 8:4-8.

Marriage as a Sacrament is a visible sign of an invisible reality. That reality is God's love. Sacramental love embodies mutual self-giving and can be defined by four traits: free, total, faithful, and fruitful. We all innately long for the fulfillment of this call and anyone who has been married has certainly also experientially understood the significant cost and daily sacrifice required to bring it to fruition.

Sex has been so distorted in our culture. The culture has attempted to cheapen it, to dismiss its power, and to undermine its purpose. I think many people read with surprise the Church's and God's view on the gift of sex. Read CCC 2362: "sexuality is a source of joy and pleasure" is some of what is mentioned if you need a little motivation to open your *Catechism*!

God gives us good gifts! I think back to the Garden of Eden and how He gave our first parents everything. The only exception was to not eat the fruit from one tree. We as humans must recognize and accept our limits. It has taken a lot of prayer and life experience to comprehend this truth, and appreciate the gift in it as well. I have come to understand that these limitations help us to not fall into selfishness and all the other vices that might tempt our total gift of self in love. When properly ordered, under God's loving divine plan and blessing, the sexual embrace can unite two persons. This makes it the closest union this side of heaven.

During a conversation with a priest friend I was struck with an interesting thought. "Imagine the power to combat evil if every married couple fully understood the magnitude of the gift God gave in the sexual embrace and all at once united this gift for the reparation of sin across the world." Well, he let out a huge belly laugh, so I'm not sure it is theologically sound, but I still wonder at the thought...

Continue reading CCC 2363, which is a deeply profound paragraph said with fatherly wisdom and purpose. Fidelity is the absolute constancy of being faithful; through good times and bad, sickness and health, and to honor one another until death. The irony here is most of us said these words at our wedding with no concept as to the depth and sacrifice required in that bold pledge.

My hope in this book is that those who are not yet married will have a headstart in understanding these truths and teachings. While we will never be fully prepared for the challenges and surprises that married love requires and offers, the sooner we can begin to understand and train ourselves, the more apt we will be to navigate these waters when the time comes.

This call of fidelity which includes unconditional love, sacrificial self-giving, and constant death to self is essential for the Sacrament of Marriage to be fully realized. When we absolutely feel confident in our partner's fidelity to us, we can more fully reveal our hearts. We can more readily open our hearts to them in vulnerability to assist in healing our areas of brokenness. Through this we can more fully enter into the relationship with each other and God that is our destiny.

The second obligation of conjugal love within the Sacrament of Marriage is fecundity, otherwise defined as procreation. Read CCC 2366 which explains the importance that children spring forth "from the very heart of that mutual giving, as its fruit and fulfillment."

In CCC 2367 the Church goes on to explain, "spouses share in the creative power and fatherhood of God." This is an amazing gift and I can tell you from my own experience, having children has helped me better understand the love of Our Father more than any other relationship. The creation, birth, care, and sacrifice required in rearing children gives me a glimpse into the unique love the Father has for each of us. It is a fascinating responsibility, that even though I fail often, I try to keep at the forefront of my mind.

CCC 2367 continues on to say, "Married couples should regard it as their proper mission to transmit human life and to educate their children; they should realize that they are thereby cooperating with the love of God the Creator and are, in a certain sense, its interpreters." This assertion that the Creator of all things has willed for us to cooperate and interpret His love for each other is so humbling, powerful, and empowering.

Regulation of Procreation

The evil one will raise his ugly head in so many distortions of this gift. One such way I've witnessed this distortion is being asked, "So are you just supposed to be a baby-making machine?" The Church again has a compassionate and realistic heart guiding us with a gentle instructive hand. The *Catechism's* eloquence in addressing this concern in CCC 2368 is so striking.

There are real conversations and considerations married couples need to have regarding children. God enters into our humanity through Jesus Christ and understands everything about our particular situations and circumstances. Care and concern for both the mental and physical health of both parents as well as children already in the home are always of concern. We have to be careful to not allow the temptation and tendency through concupiscence to let us be deceived into selfishness in our decisions.

Periodic continence, also referred to as NFP (natural family planning), comes into play here. Husbands and wives need to be aware and in tune with their bodies. CCC 2370 reminds us that "these methods respect the bodies of spouses, encourage tenderness between them, and favor the education of an authentic freedom." When we employ these methods, more intimate communication occurs between spouses. This creates even greater intimacy and love by truly seeing and knowing one another.

This has certainly been my experience in marriage once we came to understand this teaching more fully. Through admittedly awkward conversations in the beginning, my husband is now much more aware and attuned to me and vice versa. We are able to connect in non-sexual ways during times of periodic continence that build our intimacy with each other beyond the bedroom. That ironically converts to even greater intimacy in the bedroom.

Natural family planning is sensible and life-giving. Contrarily, any action to directly avoid procreation with artificial means is intrinsically evil as noted in CCC 2370. "Every action which, whether in anticipation of the conjugal act, or in its accomplishment, or in the development of its natural consequences, proposes, whether as an end or as a means, to render procreation impossible is intrinsically evil."

Direct sterilization and contraception are thus not morally acceptable. Again, the evil one raises his voice in these assertions. To which we have to remind ourselves of the four pledges of marriage: free, total, faithful and fruitful. Direct sterilization (vasectomy, hysterectomy) that are not medically necessary are contrary to those four pledges. In these situations you are not really giving yourself freely, totally, faithfully, nor fruitfully. The same can be said for contraception.

All of these in reality create a breeding ground for using the other and not fully living how we were created and designed. While it was a bit jarring, I really appreciated the analogy Fr. Mike Schmitz used in his podcast on this subject. He used the example of the choice between waiting for grandma to die or directly suffocating her. The end result is the same; she dies. However, one is the natural course of life, the other choice is murder.[33] Working with natural infertility is different than purposefully choosing infertility. Everything in your marriage will be more life-giving when both husband and wife live out their pledge of free, total, faithful, and fruitful.

The Gift of a Child

Here the Church consoles those married couples who find they cannot have children. The Church laments and suffers with them. In these circumstances, the Church helps us understand the principles within which we can operate in God's design. Not all couples are able to conceive, yet each and every sexual act needs to remain ordered to the procreation of human life even if it does not come to fruition.

Children are a gift from God and thus have integrity and rights. Because a child is not something owed to one, but is a gift, we must protect the dignity of the child and let it be at the forefront of all decisions.

The creation of a child is intrinsically connected to the sexual act. Therefore there is a huge boundary and protection of children required to preserve the sexual act for the dignity of the act and persons. Read both CCC 2375 and 2376 that address these particular protections for children and their innate rights.

Surrogate parenthood and artificial insemination are gravely immoral. They separate the procreative act from the unity act. In our society we focus so much on the couples' desire for children, but forget that we aren't owed a child. Children are a gift from God. A child is not a piece of property; it is not a right. Only the child possesses genuine rights; to be the fruit of the conjugal act, and to be respected. Children indeed have the right to be the fruit of their mother and father's love.

33 https://www.youtube.com/watch?v=v20Vg6CR9D0

Spouses who suffer infertility indeed carry a heavy cross. We are invited in all of our crosses and sufferings to unite ourselves to the Lord's Cross. In these particular circumstances of infertility, adoption or generosity of service is the way they can love. I have witnessed several friends heroically bear these crosses, adopt children and love them as their own. Fittingly, we too are adopted sons and daughters of our Lord. It is a great gift indeed.

Adultery

We continue on to the offenses against the dignity of marriage; specifically adultery and divorce. These sins, like all sins, affect the entire body of Christ and more acutely the family, children, and society at large. Adultery is one of the most destructive sins to our dignity as explained in CCC 2380-2381.

Adultery is one of the evil one's greatest tricks. He knows breaking the marriage bond is a destructive blow that can wreak havoc on families for generations to come. Jesus condemns any and every kind of adultery. Adultery can be understood as using someone in any way. Adultery is marital infidelity. Adultery is idolatry. Adultery is an injustice. When two people make a promise to each other and then break that promise, it is a sin against justice. On our wedding day, we promise fidelity for good times and bad, sickness and health, and to honor each other until death.

Every marriage will have bad times. In fact, sometimes entire seasons are filled with much suffering and brokenness. It is this broken and wounded world in which we live that we are called to help redeem. The goal of marriage is to get the other person to heaven. That means that in those bad times, arguments, disagreements, stress, and brokenness we must hold firmly to our vow. Sacramental marriages have the help of the Holy Spirit to pour out mercy, grace, forgiveness, and help create hearts willing to sacrifice, change, and amend for the good of the other.

This effort takes prudence, temperance, and other virtues, as well as a disciplined mindset to not allow your feelings to take control. Sometimes we may be inclined to engage in certain behaviors because of our feelings, yet we are called to acknowledge those passions and put them under submission to our intellect and will. If you experience the temptations of adultery in your marriage, please communicate them to the Lord in prayer and to a confessor. Powerful conversions happen when we light up the darkness. There can be many underlying reasons and/or triggers and you owe it to yourself and your spouse to uncover them. The Lord offers abundant mercy and help. We have to do our part to acknowledge our weakness and take accountability and prudent action to work with the Lord's grace.

Divorce

In many cases, adultery is a primary cause of divorce. Divorce is a grave offense against the natural law and does injury to the covenant of salvation. CCC 2385 highlights why divorce is such a serious sin:

> **2385** Divorce is immoral also because it introduces disorder into the family and into society. This disorder brings grave harm to the deserted spouse, to children traumatized by the separation of their parents and often torn between them, and because of its contagious effect which makes it truly a plague on society.

Divorce greatly impacts children. It removes all certainty and security in their home environment. It wounds them not only in their childhood but well into their adult lives and also impacts their future choices. The Church recognizes that there is a considerable difference between the one who leaves and the one who is left in the marriage. It also recognizes that the separation of spouses can be legitimate for safety or other serious reasons, yet the couple remains married during this separation. We must take all opportunities to ensure we teach our young people the absolute importance and gravity of entering into marriage and the beauty contained there within.

Many of us were not well formed going into marriage. This puts those couples at a disadvantage and likewise makes the journey much more difficult. However, notwithstanding any danger or abuse, fighting for your marriage is always a worthy endeavor. I have a friend currently going through the annulment process. He shared with me a perspective that made a huge impression on me. He said, "our marriage was really hard. We had many challenges to overcome. But I'll tell you what, divorce and all of the ramifications that come with it are even harder. I implore anyone I know and love to fight to the death for their marriage." A phrase I heard recently seems very applicable, "The grass is greener where you water it."

Please consider praying this prayer with me: *God, give me the grace to recognize that marriage is a Sacrament of service designed to help my spouse get to Heaven. Help me to die to self, pick up my cross, lean into your wisdom and your will. Pour your grace into our marriage so that we may be your visible sign of love to the world.*

If you have experienced the wound of divorce, know that the Church acknowledges the pain and suffering associated with it. She offers support to navigate this difficult experience. Please consider praying this prayer with me: *God, give me the grace and divine assistance to help me seek spiritual guidance, to find healing through faith and community, and be encouraged to participate in the life of the Church.*

Other Sins Against Marriage

The final section of the *Catechism* instructs about other offenses against the dignity of marriage that are perhaps a little less common. Polygamy, incest, sexual abuse, and free union are all grave sins against marriage. For non-Christians who live in polygamy and want to convert, the Gospel cannot change, but people can change and adapt to what the Church teaches. They are called to align their lives in accordance with the moral law. They must change their ways, yet also honor the obligations of the former way of life and responsibilities. This can be very complex to navigate but ultimately accomplished.

Incest designates intimate relations between relatives or in-laws within a degree that prohibits marriage between them. It corrupts family relationships and marks a regression toward animality. Connected to incest is any sexual abuse perpetrated by adults on children or adolescents entrusted to their care. The offense is compounded by the scandalous harm done to the physical and moral integrity of the young, who will remain scarred by it all their lives, and the violation of responsibility for their upbringing.

Free-union, also known as cohabitation, is fallacious. There is a lack of trust, security, and an unstable future in these situations. There is no commitment to fidelity and we are called to reject cohabitation. I mentioned earlier the statistics support cohabitation equates to high divorce rates. It is foolish to think we can have trial marriages because marriages are in definition permanent. Human love does not tolerate trial marriages. People don't want to be "tried out." It demands a total and definitive gift to one another. Saint John Paul II said, "the person who does not decide to love forever will find it very difficult to really love for even one day."[34]

This is the longest and arguably the most exacting Commandment. Congratulations for completing it. You made it! I invite you to set the book down and spend some time in prayer. Ask the Lord what He wants to impart to you about all that you have read.

---

34 https://www.catholic.com/magazine/online-edition/eight-things-you-have-to-know-about-the-churchs-teaching-on-divorce?ref=farodefe.org

Reflection Questions

Take some time to reflect upon the questions below. Consider writing in your Reconciliation journal or notebook of your choice. Invite the Lord to be present with you as you consider these questions.

- *What thoughts or feelings surfaced when reading this chapter?*
- *Did anything stand out to you as new or different than you had previously considered?*
- *Did the Lord convict your heart in a particular way?*
- *Are you moved to repent?*
- *Did you receive any interior movement in your heart, a consolation, or a deeper love for God or neighbor?*
- *What do you want to ask the Lord for now?*

Examination of Conscience—Sixth Commandment

Now that we have explored the Sixth Commandment, perhaps in greater detail than you have before, I invite you to sit with the Lord and review the following questions. What is the Lord saying to you? Holy Spirit Come!

1. *Have I taken the necessary precautions to safeguard my purity and my faith?*
2. *Have I given in to lust—by a disordered desire for or inordinate enjoyment of sexual pleasure isolated from its procreative and unitive purposes?*
3. *Have I seduced someone or allowed myself to be seduced?*
4. *Have I made unwelcomed or uninvited sexual advances towards another?*
5. *Have I purposely dressed immodestly?*
6. *Have I engaged in masturbation, fornication, or premarital sex?*
7. *Have I engaged in foreplay outside the context of marriage?*

8. *Have I engaged in foreplay within the context of marriage but not ordered to the procreative and unitive function of sex?*

9. *Have I purchased, viewed or made use of pornography, or participated in the creation, sale or engagement of it?*

10. *Have I engaged in prostitution?*

11. *Have I participated in any form or the condoning of rape?*

12. *Have I preyed upon children or youth for my sexual pleasure?*

13. *Have I engaged in impurity and immodesty in words, looks, and actions, whether alone or with others through impure jokes, music, television, movies, books, or on the internet?*

14. *Have I caused scandal by living together before marriage?*

15. *Have I engaged in homosexual activity?*

16. *Have I participated in immoral techniques that entail the dissociation of husband and wife—sperm or egg donation, surrogate uterus, artificial insemination, or in vitro fertilization?*

17. *Have I sinned against the dignity of marriage through adultery, divorce, polygamy, incest, or free unions?*

CHAPTER SEVEN

The Seventh Commandment—You Shall Not Steal

Prior to intentionally studying the Commandments, the Seventh Commandment is one that perhaps I'd given the least amount of attention to in my life personally. However, delving into Church teaching about it opened a treasure trove. It calls to mind the tension between the two concepts of universal destination of goods and the private ownership of goods. This helps us understand that we have the right to private property and at the same time a call to embody a mindset and heart of stewardship.

Always using these earthly possessions and talents for the greater good helps us walk the tightrope of integrity. We are invited to view everything we have and everything we are given through a God lens as pure gift. We are invited to gratefully receive these gifts ranging from time, intellect, talent, money, and resources as that: gifts. Gifts that we are stewards of and not owners of. Everything we have been given including the very breath we take is given to us by God. A commitment to this mindset helps us navigate this Commandment freely. In a nutshell, the Seventh Commandment prohibits theft, which usurps another's property against the reasonable will of the owner. This concept is much broader than I was first inclined to think.

Using What We Have Well

The opening paragraph in the *Catechism* sets the stage very well. I invite you to read CCC 2401-2402.

God is good to us and generous in His design. He created all these wonderful resources and has given us access to, and a responsibility for, all which is ordered for our flourishing. In His design, as the final sentence in 2402 suggests, this benevolence "should allow for a natural solidarity to develop between man." God created everything we need, gave it to us freely out of love, for us to love and care for one another. It is what makes sins against this Commandment so destructive. Our sin and selfishness create an environment where entire regions of people go without food or basic necessities while others live in opulence with perhaps not enough generosity to reach out to the less fortunate.

My husband and I spent a couple of years praying and trying to decide whether or not to build a pool. For those of you who live in the South, the heat almost makes it a necessity. In fact, when you fly over Dallas-Fort Worth in an airplane, this claim is made quite visual when you see so many houses with blue kidney bean shapes in their backyards. What made this decision so hard for us was the sheer expense of a pool. We have generally lived frugally out of the sense that we are stewards and not owners of what we've been given. Many can debate what a good steward looks like. It can involve many choices including what schools to send your children to, field of employment to enter, and number of hours worked. All of these can result in certain "rights" that come with the effort we put into our jobs and work. My husband and I simply choose to work hard, be grateful for what we have, and know it could all be taken away in an instant (a debilitating long-term illness, losing a job, or other unforeseen situation).

As we deliberated this decision we chose to take a few small steps. First we bought an inexpensive above-ground pool. Well that burst within the first few weeks so we moved on to a higher quality, somewhat substantial sized above-ground pool. I remember I told my husband that the laughter seemed to sound the same in that pool versus when we swam in my parents' in-ground pool. So perhaps this nice above-ground pool was our answer.

Almost as soon as I committed that thought to my heart, something else happened. I went to a beautiful Catholic conference. I brought this specific prayer with me to Adoration at the conference. During the presentation following Adoration, one of the presenters talked about Family Nights. They described it as a time set aside to invite people over to socialize and fellowship with one another on a regular basis. No sooner than I heard their description I heard the Lord say, "this is what I want for you."

The concept of Sanchez Summer Nights was born that day. We made the decision to spend the money to build a substantial in-ground pool and create a gathering space for the Lord's work. We recently completed our fifth annual Sanchez Summer Nights. What started as a small community of friends has blossomed into sometimes upwards of 75 neighbors, friends, and clergy gathering every Friday in summer to celebrate and enjoy doing life together. It has taught my kids how to prepare (lots of cleaning!), and how to be gracious hosts. It has shown us that there is abundant blessing to not hoard what we have but freely offer it in a responsible and prayerfully discerned way.

CCC 2404 invites us to understand the Church's position about how we use things. For me, it was a sweet little signal grace from God affirming our decision about our pool project and the future use of it.

We belong to each other. Wouldn't you know that the literal week our pool construction project finished the entire world shut down due to Covid. I felt like the Lord said to me, "Carrie, the first year of use of this pool and outdoor space is for your family to enjoy intimately together, and then I'll invite you to share it openly with others." I felt so grateful for this sweet little gift from the Lord to our family.

I love that one of my more reserved friends has told me that Sanchez Summer Nights has been such a blessing to their family. They are much more introverted and while they know they need community, the thought of orchestrating such an event is much too overwhelming for them. They have expressed to us how opening our home in this way has been such a gift to their family. This ability, borne out of a stewardship mentality, is a beautiful display of giving and receiving freely. It is really such a gift in so many ways!

The Church teaches that we need the virtue of temperance, and practice of justice and solidarity, especially in regards to this Commandment. Offenses against the Seventh Commandment include:

- deliberate retention of goods lent or objects lost
- business fraud
- paying unjust wages
- forcing up prices by taking advantage of ignorance or hardship of another (payday loans).

Additional offenses include:

- morally illicit-speculation
- manipulating prices
- corruption to influence judgment
- bribery
- use for private purposes of common good
- work poorly done
- tax evasion
- forgery of checks and invoices
- excessive expenses or waste
- willfully damaging public or private property

Promises and Contracts

I learned something completely new in reading this section of the *Catechism* which helped me feel a sense of relief from a burden I didn't realize I carried. CCC 2410 discusses promises and contracts.

Reading that section brought me back to when my husband and I were about to be married. We were young, hopeful, and filled with excitement for all the adventures that awaited us, including purchasing our first home together. We found the perfect little house. It had everything we were looking for, and the price was right!

We signed all the contracts and passed all the necessary inspections. We were so excited to start this new chapter in our lives. Well six days before closing we received a call from our realtor. She told us that the sellers decided not to sell to us. There was some speculation that racism was a factor. We were stunned. This was illegal! This wasn't fair! We had already put in a notice to each one of our apartment complexes. We had nearly everything boxed up and movers were arranged! How could this be?

Again, we were thrust into prayer about how to handle this situation. We decided to pursue justice. It was a gut-wrenching couple of months. We had to hire an attorney, which we had no experience in. We continually questioned our decision. We wondered what we had done to provoke such a change from the sellers. I developed an ulcer from all the stress.

We finally received our court date to hopefully put all of this behind us. Again, six days before the court date, the sellers dropped all roadblocks and agreed to sell us the home. They were on the hook for not only all of our attorney's fees, moving and storage fees, but also their own attorney's fees and expenses. What an expensive mess and hardship all the way around. We may never know the reason behind this experience but it certainly was an illustration of God's Commandments at work in a very practical and real way.

The Church confirms that all injustices require reparation. Commutative justice regulates exchanges between persons and institutions. Legal justice is what a citizen owes in fairness to the community. Distributive justice is what the community owes its citizens. Reparative Justice has to come from our hearts.

The law is limited. If the sellers had come to us with whatever their concerns were, they would have given us the opportunity to have compassion on whatever their situation was that dictated a change. We likely would have understood and avoided all of the stress and drama that ensued. We attempted to enter into these conversations with them to no avail. For me it squarely showed me how when we operate within God's Commandments, the opportunity for peace and human flourishing is so much more possible than when we choose selfishness or to go our own way.

In the final section of "respect for the goods of others" it discusses that gambling is not in itself contrary to justice unless it deprives someone of their necessities or causes someone to become addicted. Cheating at games constitutes grave matter unless the damage is insignificant. We are card and board game players and we often remind ourselves of this teaching. While one may certainly say losing to a cheater at Monopoly is insignificant, my family might give you a run for your money in that debate! Finally, any acts or enterprises that lead to the enslavement of people are always wrong.

Respect for Creation

We continue in the section dedicated to respect for the integrity of creation. We are reminded that as stewards of Creation we must look at our relationship and responsibility for those with which we were given dominion, specifically animals.

Animals' existence glorifies God, therefore we owe them kindness. God has entrusted animals to our stewardship. It is legitimate to use animals for food, clothing, and pets. Medical and scientific experimentation is morally acceptable if it remains within reasonable limits, and contributes to the care or saving of human lives. It is contrary to human dignity to cause animals to suffer or die needlessly.

The Church gives us a sense of order for how to regard animals and be good stewards. While we love our animals, we must consider the balance and priority of money spent. We are invited to consider if it's worthy to spend money on animals instead of the relief of human misery.

Social Responsibilities

It is under the Seventh Commandment that the Church highlights the need for Catholic Social Doctrines. Because the Church was given the full revelation of the truth about man from the Gospels, her greatest responsibility is "to bear witness to man, in the name of Christ, to his dignity and his vocation to the communion of persons. She teaches him the demands of justice and peace in conformity with divine wisdom" (CCC 2419).

I really appreciate the explanation of the Church's role in society, especially in today's age when we hear so much about separation of church and state. I am thankful to have an entity, Mother Church, who is inspired by the Holy Spirit to treat all of mankind with dignity and respect. Even in my own limited lifetime I have seen so much abuse of power in big and small matters alike. While the Church may be flawed in the humans that comprise it, I am genuinely grateful that we have our Creator who operates outside of time and space to guide us in timeless principles. These truths continue to prove to me the consistency in logic and reason independent of any "religiosity," even if at first I may not understand or even be inclined to disagree with the principles presented.

The Church is alive and while the fullness of revelation has been completed through Jesus, Mother Church continues to offer her loving instruction as mankind continues to mature and develop. The

Industrial Revolution ignited a need for the Church to establish Social Doctrine to guide mankind with the advent of new technologies and temptations. CCC 2421 helps to clarify why this need was so pressing. Take a moment to read it now.

Some of these new structures for the production of consumer goods and new forms of labor and ownership, created a huge opportunity for there to be a distinct imbalance and temptation to control, manipulate, and extort large groups of people. I find CCC 2424 compelling and right on target. It frames the necessity for providing this guidance.

> **2424** A theory that makes profit the exclusive norm and ultimate end of economic activity is morally unacceptable. The disordered desire for money cannot but produce perverse effects. It is one of the causes of the many conflicts which disturb the social order.
>
> A system that "subordinates the basic rights of individuals and of groups to the collective organization of production" is contrary to human dignity. Every practice that reduces persons to nothing more than a means of profit enslaves man, leads to idolizing money, and contributes to the spread of atheism. "You cannot serve God and mammon."

The Church offers her wisdom in anticipation of the potential for work to become dehumanizing. It is a fallacious basis to define our identity by our work. This is very dangerous territory. When we bring this large-scale view into a personal focus, it can show us at the core how destructive these principles can be.

For instance, how many of us grew up in homes that, intentionally or not, were defined by "what we did" instead of "who we are?" Many of us were likely raised with an expectation that we had to be successful academically, athletically, and socially to have value. This may have been subtly reinforced when we were praised for what we did, or perhaps punished for what we didn't do or didn't do well. There are many of my dear friends, faithful Christians and non-Christians alike, who are currently in therapy. They are trying to understand how this mentality colored their perspective and lives. This flawed understanding of identity can be a barrier to receive the free gift of God's unconditional love and our true identity as adopted sons and daughters.

When we return to the large-scale view, no wonder the Church is adamant that communism and socialism are not to be accepted. Capitalism, for its part, must be held in close supervision to always promote the entire humans' dignity and disallow an environment of valuing money over people. CCC 2425 explains in further detail. Please read it now.

Work and Economics

The Church continues to be a voice of clarity in this complex world. She is careful to walk the very tight rope protecting human dignity at all costs. She also reminds us that work is both a gift and a responsibility. Again I appreciate the sentiment wonderfully expressed in CCC 2427:

> **2427** *Human work* proceeds directly from persons created in the image of God and called to prolong the work of creation by subduing the earth, both with and for one another. Hence work is a duty: "If any one will not work, let him not eat." Work honors the Creator's gifts and the talents received from him. It can also be redemptive. By enduring the hardship of work in union with Jesus, the carpenter of Nazareth and the one crucified on Calvary, man collaborates in a certain fashion with the Son of God in his redemptive work. He shows himself to be a disciple of Christ by carrying the cross, daily, in the work he is called to accomplish. Work can be a means of sanctification and a way of animating earthly realities with the Spirit of Christ.

Work allows us to express our creativity and utilize the very specific and unique gifts that God has given each one of us. One of the most rewarding experiences of motherhood is to watch and nourish gifts that emerge in my children. I recall my oldest daughter's All-State choir competition experiences throughout high school. Her sophomore year she poured herself into hours of rehearsals, practice, and training. She was rewarded for her effort by making the All-State choir. Her junior year was similar with a similar result.

Her senior year took a different turn. Although we didn't track the hours, she likely spent as much time and effort or more on learning the music and honing her sight reading skills. However, leading up to the competition, there was something markedly different. In the two previous years her stomach and mind were filled with anxiety about the results. We had many conversations about always putting in your best effort and striving for excellence in all that you do, but being aware to never allow yourself to fall into the temptation trap of wrapping your identity in a specific result.

In the two previous years we'd go into her final auditions with the belief and understanding that God already knew the outcome. We talked about the choice to believe that His word is true in Romans 8:28. "We know that all things work for good for those who love God, who are called according to his purpose." The phrase, "strive for excellence but release the results to God" is commonly spoken in our home. God knows what we need and knows what will be most edifying for our journey. Trust Him.

Her senior year, the pressure was on. She was a two year All-Stater already, choir president, and the weight of achievement was squarely on her shoulders. She came out of her audition cautiously confident and at peace. However, she did not make the final cut. This result would more than likely crush some kids. She was disappointed for sure, but she carried a peace and acceptance with her that was palpable. She faced the shock and comments of her classmates with confidence that while this certainly was something she wanted and worked to achieve, she also sensed that there was a reason and a purpose in her not achieving this goal. She expressed her gratitude and appreciation for the two previous years' "successful" experiences equally as her "unsuccessful" senior year. She could do this because she was firmly rooted in her identity as a beloved daughter and not because of her achievements.

Some may think this example is quite a stretch from the intent of this Commandment but I think it actually helps crystallize the importance of understanding "work is for man, not man for work" (CCC 2428). While auditioning for a high school singing competition is not work in the traditional sense of going to a job and receiving payment, it does illustrate how much our current society can dangerously reorient the focus and purpose of work to the detriment of human dignity. God has presented that all work is "ordered first of all to the service of persons, of the whole man, and of the entire human community" (CCC 2426).

For those business leaders of our community, the *Catechism* offers some practical guidance in CCC 2432-2436. If you are a business leader, it would benefit you to read those paragraphs in detail. In summary, we must strive to maintain the delicate balance between the universal destination of goods and the respect for the right to private property.

Specifically in the United States, as a wealthy nation, we have an added responsibility and duty of solidarity, charity, and justice to support nations who are unable to fully ensure their own development. There is ample discussion about the different strategies to achieve this end. There must be solidarity with nations and we need to work against perverse mechanisms that keep poor countries poor. We must always advocate and support endeavors that will improve human society.

We must extend the same principles we employ from our one-on-one interactions to societies at large as best we can. If I have a friend in need, I can offer what I am able, to help alleviate their need as best I can. Simultaneously I can work with them to improve any long-term underlying conditions that contribute to the problem. Again the Church communicates principles, not policy, to creatively explore to the benefit of the greater good of all of humanity. There are certainly complex issues at hand but when we undertake any issue with a heart of authentic love and charity, real solutions are bound to follow.

Care for the Poor

The final section in the *Catechism* about the Seventh Commandment, wraps up with love of the poor. Scripture is laced with references to the dangers of riches as well as our call to love and care for the poor. CCC 2444 highlights our responsibility:

> **2444** "The Church's love for the poor . . . is a part of her constant tradition." This love is inspired by the Gospel of the Beatitudes, of the poverty of Jesus, and of his concern for the poor. Love for the poor is even one of the motives for the duty of working so as to "be able to give to those in need." It extends not only to material poverty but also to the many forms of cultural and religious poverty.

Loving the poor is part of God's divine justice that we give to everyone that which is their due. All of His children are due human dignity, respect, and loving care. We cannot go through this life ignorant of those in need. When we are truly filled with love of God we will not be unaware of the plight of our neighbor.

At a very close friend's funeral they chose Matthew 25:35-45. My favorite parallel lines in that selection are "Amen, I say to you, whatever you did for one of these least brothers of mine, you did for me," juxtaposed against "Amen, I say to you, what you did not do for one of these least ones, you did not do for me." St. Gregory the Great reminds us in CCC 2446, "when we attend to the needs of those in want, we give them what is theirs, not ours. More than performing works of mercy, we are paying a debt of justice."

As a Church we are blessed with the beauty and duty to perform both spiritual and corporal works of mercy that are incumbent on us all. CCC 2447 defines these works of mercy:

> **2447** The *works of mercy* are charitable actions by which we come to the aid of our neighbor in his spiritual and bodily necessities. Instructing, advising, consoling, comforting are spiritual works of mercy, as are forgiving and bearing wrongs patiently. The corporal works of mercy consist especially in feeding the hungry, sheltering the homeless, clothing the naked, visiting the sick and imprisoned, and burying the dead. Among all these, giving alms to the poor is one of the chief witnesses to fraternal charity: it is also a work of justice pleasing to God...

What I love about our Church and the Seventh Commandment is that it has something for everyone. There were times in our early married life where we did not have much in the way of financial resources. Yet, that did not let us off the hook to provide for the poor among us. While in those early years we weren't able to provide in financially substantial ways, we gave of our time, energy, and talent.

One of the most beautiful treasures that developed in those years was a love to sing at funerals. Many people look at me sideways when I say that, but for me it is one of the most raw opportunities to pour love and comfort into those in need. As I have matured in faith, my prayer now before every funeral is 'please Lord, take over my voice and allow it to be your love for this family.' Every time someone graciously compliments or offers gratitude for my singing after the funeral, I take the opportunity to share with them my secret. I tell them of the prayer, and if they allow me, I wrap them in a hug as a vessel to feel the loving embrace of the Father.

Reflection Questions

Take some time to reflect upon the questions below. Consider writing in your Reconciliation journal or notebook of your choice. Invite the Lord to be present with you as you consider these questions.

- *What thoughts or feelings surfaced when reading this chapter?*
- *Did anything stand out to you as new or different than you had previously considered?*
- *Did the Lord convict your heart in a particular way?*
- *Are you moved to repent?*
- *Did you receive any interior movement in your heart, a consolation, or a deeper love for God or neighbor?*
- *What do you want to ask the Lord for now?*

Examination of Conscience—Seventh Commandment

Now that we have explored the Seventh Commandment, perhaps in greater detail than you have before, I invite you to sit with the Lord and review the following questions. What is the Lord saying to you? Holy Spirit Come!

1. *Have I stolen?*
2. *Have I neglected to live in a spirit of Gospel poverty and simplicity?*
3. *Have I neglected to give generously to others in need?*
4. *Have I forgotten to consider that God has provided me with money so that I might use it to benefit others, as well as for my own legitimate needs?*
5. *Have I allowed myself to be overly consumeristic?*
6. *Have I appreciated the dignity of work and made legitimate and good use of my talents?*
7. *Have I participated in the manipulation of prices, corruption, tax evasion, insurance fraud, or forgery of checks or invoices?*
8. *Have I deliberately defaced, destroyed, or lost another's property?*
9. *Have I cheated on a test, taxes, sports, games, or in business?*
10. *Have I squandered money in compulsive gambling?*
11. *Do I pay my employees fairly?*
12. *Have I failed to honor my part of a contract?*
13. *Have I failed to make good on a debt?*
14. *Have I overcharged someone, especially to take advantage of another's hardship or ignorance?*
15. *Have I misused or overindulged in natural resources?*
16. *Have I neglected to practice the corporal works of mercy?*
17. *Have I neglected to practice the spiritual works of mercy?*

CHAPTER EIGHT

The Eighth Commandment—You Shall Not Bear False Witness

The *Catechism* chapter on the Eighth Commandment opens up with a succinct summary. Read CCC 2464 and 2465 now.

The deeper I traverse the depths of our Catholic faith, the more in awe I become of God and His great love and Providence for us. These days I cannot tell you how many times I hear "my truth, your truth." What a misconception and outright lie.

John 17:17 declares, "Consecrate them in the truth. Your word is truth." This verse is part of a larger conversation between Jesus and God the Father, aptly called the "high priestly prayer" of Jesus. What an incredible gift given to the disciples and then us, when we overhear the prayer of Jesus to His Father. You can feel the intimacy and authenticity of what is expressed when you read John 17 in its entirety.

We live in a time where we have instant access to information. It's comical to remember when I had to painstakingly pull out the thick thesaurus or dictionary to look up words. Now you can find endless quotes, memes, and definitions with the click of a button. Now teachers and professors have to send students' essays through an AI detection app to see if the words were the students' own or not.

The danger in all of this information so easily accessible, is that it is also easily manipulated to achieve one's own agenda and desires. To me it is further evidence and encouragement that we can stand in solidarity with Scripture and Church teaching that has existed for thousands of years. It has been proclaimed and evidenced throughout time, revolutions, and history: God is the source of all truth.

You can take any number of popular topics and have as many opinions as stars in the sky. Truthfulness is a virtue which consists of showing oneself as true in deed and truthful in words. It also requires us to guard against duplicity, dissimulation, and hypocrisy. In order to be in a relationship, we have to have mutual confidence that we are being truthful to each other. "Let your yes be yes and your no be no" (James 5:12). This is the goal. Unfortunately every single human I have ever interacted with has failed me. And I have failed them. This is reality due to our weaknesses.

That leaves my heart desiring something much more solid and pure than mankind to place my trust. I need solid grounding. As Jesus speaks in Matthew 7:24-29:

> Everyone who listens to these words of mine and acts on them will be like a wise man who built his house on rock. The rain fell, the floods came, and the winds blew and buffeted the houses. But it did not collapse; it had been set solidly on rock. And everyone who listens to these words of mine but does not act on them will be like a fool who built his house on sand. The rain fell, the floods came, and the winds blew and buffeted the house. And it collapsed and was completely ruined." When Jesus finished these words, the crowds were astonished at his teaching, for he taught them as one having authority, and not as their scribes.

In every one of my experiences, God's word ends up as Truth. I often struggle through apparent contradictions between my perspective and God's. Sometimes those are very long seasons of wrestling. Ultimately however, the words spoken in Isaiah 55:9 ring true, "For as the heavens are higher than the earth, so are my ways higher than your ways, my thoughts higher than your thoughts." Death, sickness, arguments, hurts, disappointments...all can be understood in the light of God's Word.

Live in the Truth

Once we know this truth, we are called as disciples of Christ to "live in the truth." Our actions, words, and deeds must always bear witness to the truth of our faith.

Sometimes we can become squeamish in this regard. We feel ill equipped, scared, or fall victim to the notion that evangelization means we cram our beliefs down someone's throat. My hope is that this book gives you confidence to think, talk, and act towards our faith differently. I pray you have encountered the Lord. I hope you feel a sense of love and excitement to know you are not witnesses to hollow rules, but rather love letters from a God who loves you immensely; and is the Truth.

We have great witnesses in the martyrs and saints that have gone before us. They have testified to this truth. It is no easy task. I am thankful for their witness. It has strengthened my own faith and provided me proof that others also see what I see in my eyes of faith. The Saints risked their lives to safeguard and advance the mission of the Gospel.

Some of you might be familiar with Charles "Chuck" Colson's testimony of Watergate proving Christ's Resurrection. In a nutshell, Mr. Colson was an assistant to Richard Nixon and convicted for his involvement in the Watergate scandal. He admittedly reported that even though he was an expert in cover-ups, those who were involved only lasted

12 days under the pressure of investigation before they admitted the truth. He and the other men involved were among the most powerful people at the time. An admission of guilt would merely be a source of embarrassment and potential prison time, not a death sentence.

The stakes were not even life threatening and yet they quickly caved to the pressure. Colson compared himself to the disciples. The disciples were 12 powerless men, peasants. They faced not only embarrassment or political disgrace, but beatings, stonings, and ultimately execution. Not one of them denied what they saw. They testified to the truth to the end.

I love being challenged by the question: if Christianity became illegal, would they have enough evidence to convict me of being a Christian? One of the greatest compliments I've received is from a lady I met through a bible study. After hearing me speak in our small group about one of my encounters with the Lord, she stopped me, looked at me quizzically and said, "you really know HIM, don't you?" What a gift that my interior relationship with the Lord was externally visible. I am so grateful for my very intimate and powerful relationship with the Lord. And yet, this living relationship is not just for the few—He wants that with you!

Please pray with me: *Lord, continue to pour out your grace of courage into all of our hearts that we are convicted that you are the Truth and we can confidently proclaim your Gospel of Love and Truth. Impress upon our minds and our hearts that all you have spoken is truth. This world wants to convince us otherwise. Help us to be steadfast and trust your Word.*

Offenses Against Truth

Truthfulness is vital to our faith. Unfortunately that means in our weakness it is easy to sin against it. CCC 2475 calls us to "put away all falsehood, we are to 'put away all malice and all guile and insincerity and envy and all slander." Let's dive a bit further into each one of these offenses against truth as outlined in CCC 2475-2487. Below is a list of offenses followed by an explanation of each:

- False Witness
- Perjury
- Rash Judgement
- Detraction
- Calumny
- Flattery
- Adulation
- Complaisance
- Boasting or bragging
- Lying

False witness references an offense against truth publicly in court. Perjury is when a false statement is made under oath. Both of these "contribute to condemnation of the innocent, exoneration of the guilty, or the increased punishment of the accused." CCC 2477 continues with examples of other offenses against truth that perhaps are readily seen in everyday life.

As Christians we are called to presume goodwill and give the benefit of the doubt to each other. CCC 2478 encourages us to "be careful to interpret insofar as possible his neighbor's thoughts, words, and deeds in a favorable way." We have to discipline ourselves to ask for clarification if we are uncertain as to our neighbor's intention.

Sadly, I think this occurs all too often especially in marriages, including my own. How many times am I guilty of hearing what my husband says and immediately think the worst? Over time and with open communication, my husband and I have come to know each other and our individual tendencies better. Now I can recognize when he approaches me about an issue, it is not to blame or condemn, but rather to work towards a resolution that will prevent future problems.

I never previously considered how it is actually sinful to assume the moral fault of another. It has been very helpful for our communication and marriage to be more aware and disciplined in assuming each other's goodwill. Furthermore, this Commandment challenges us to consider whether or not we assume goodwill towards our children, our parents, and our co-workers. One may conclude that the extreme division we see in our nation may be a result of many sinning against this Commandment. I wonder if we all strove to improve upon this one area in a specific way, how it could help change the trajectory of our families and nation.

The *Catechism* continues on to explain that both detraction and calumny destroy the reputation and honor of one's neighbor. Detraction is when you reveal a person's real faults to another person without a valid reason. For example, there are memes about wives speaking negatively about their husbands on the soccer sidelines. Their husbands might have the real faults they speak about, but it is a sin if there is not a valid reason to disclose those faults. Venting, lamenting, or doing so to establish a weak common bond with friends are not valid reasons to reveal another's faults. This ought to be avoided.

Conversely, there are times and situations that absolutely call for you to go to a trusted, spiritually mature friend, priest, or counselor. In this scenario, when you seek advice about how to handle a particular fault of your spouse for the benefit of your marriage, it likely is not a sin of detraction. It is a careful tightrope to walk. We always do well to critically analyze our intention and motivation of discussing another's fault to determine if we sin in this particular way.

Calumny is intentionally making false and defamatory statements with the express purpose to destroy someone's reputation. Gossip is commonly the catchall phrase for these sins. Anytime we do not speak life over someone, but rather speak ill to destroy their life in some way, it is a sin. There is power in our words. We have a responsibility to have custody over our tongues and hearts. Proverbs 18:21 reminds us, "Death and life are in the power of the tongue; those who choose one shall eat its fruit."

Read CCC 2480. It discusses flattery, adulation, and complaisance in regards to supporting sinful behavior. All of these actions are sins which seek to encourage another in malicious acts. This includes participating in the sin, ordering, advising, or approving of it. It also includes not disclosing or hindering the sin, or protecting those who are engaging in some evil.

In our day and age this seems to be a common sin. We may not initially realize when we commit it. We've all heard the phrase "do whatever makes you happy." This mindset can be dangerous as it leads us to participate in the above mentioned sins. When we see our brothers and sisters commit sins, we are called to lovingly bring it to their attention. We must be on guard not to support them in their sin. This is a difficult responsibility, especially because the fact is, we are all sinners.

Matthew 7:3-5 appropriately guides us through this predicament:

> Why do you notice the splinter in your brother's eye, but do not perceive the wooden beam in your own eye? How can you say to your brother, 'Let me remove that splinter from your eye,' while the wooden beam is in your eye? You hypocrite, remove the wooden beam from your eye first; then you will see clearly to remove the splinter from your brother's eye.

This Scripture is so applicable because it reminds us that we must recognize our own sinfulness and repent. In this purified state we are then instructed to remove the splinter from our brother's eye. We have an important responsibility not to be complicit in our brother's sin nor encourage them in sin. We must instead do the demanding task of shining God's light in the darkness.

It is important to read through *Catechism* paragraphs 2482-2486 as they highlight the gravity and nuances of lying. I appreciate the eloquence and clarity in which the Church teaches.

Sarcasm is included in the category of sins against truth. The etymology of sarcasm in Greek '*sarkazein*' which means tear the flesh.

It is such a visual representation of what sarcasm can do to a person. Sarcasm can be incredibly destructive to relationships and people.

Each one of these paragraphs so clearly illustrates why truthfulness is vital and lying is destructive. The Church compassionately recognizes the variability and spectrum of culpability regarding this sin, yet also helps establish the standard to which we can measure ourselves.

To bring this to a more personal level, one of the most respected and appreciated attributes about my mom was her truthfulness. I always knew where I stood in her eyes. She told me the truth; even when it hurt my feelings. However, she also wrapped the truth in charity (love). That enabled me to live my life on solid footing. I learned how to separate my feelings from the logic and realities of the situation and make choices accordingly.

I can only imagine what my life would look like if I hadn't had someone close to me who was willing to speak the truth, even when it was difficult to hear. I am grateful for this example and gift she gave me. It is something that I have chosen to carry forward with my children. They have lamented the times I did hurt their feelings but needed to speak the hard truths to them. Though they are still young, they can already articulate their appreciation for this gift, which then becomes a gift back to me. God is so good in His wisdom and love for us in His Commandments!

On Keeping Secrets or Not Sharing Truth

Truthfulness is further expounded in the *Catechism* regarding the right to communication. We have a responsibility to prudently consider what we decide to reveal and we must always share in charity. Fraternal love dictates whether or not we reveal the truth to someone. I don't have to say everything I think or know. This takes great discernment.

A light-hearted example comes to mind. When my children were toddlers, one in particular was doing something they weren't supposed to be doing. The phrase 'small people, small problems' comes to mind. In that moment, I chose to avoid eye contact with them, effectively not communicating to them that I was aware of their misgivings. It was one of those situations where it was not prudent or effective to tell them everything I knew. That prudence protected against "nagging" and allowed for a greater instruction and teaching for their edification at a later more appropriate time.

The same can be true in 'big people' situations. Oftentimes I have witnessed certain behaviors and choices and when taken into prayer about my response, I receive instruction to "ponder" and "hold in my heart." Time and time again listening and obeying those carefully discerned decisions have borne much fruit.

One very special and unique circumstance that always falls into the category of the right to communication is within the Sacrament of Reconciliation.

> **2490** The *secret of the sacrament of reconciliation* is sacred, and cannot be violated under any pretext. "The sacramental seal is inviolable; therefore, it is a crime for a confessor in any way to betray a penitent by word or in any other manner or for any reason."

The sacramental seal is such an integral and essential element of the Sacrament of Reconciliation. I love Reconciliation so much. It has brought much freedom to my life. What do I mean by that? Certainly I am thankful for the primary purpose of reconciliation being the forgiveness of my sins. But having a sacred space where I can reveal my true heart fully, knowing that it will be held in the strictest of confidence, creates the environment for true conversion and healing of my heart. Whatever we persistently bring to the light, darkness cannot take hold.

It is such a gift to have a priest operate *in persona Christi*; meaning, in the person of Christ. It is the closest parallel we will have on this side of heaven to experience what the woman at the well experienced.

She experienced Jesus knowing all her sins. They acknowledged them together, and He loved her into conversion. For us, the Sacrament of Reconciliation offers us the gift of an anointed representative of Jesus who looks us in the eye, accompanies us on acknowledging all of our sins, witnesses our contrition and repentance, forgives our sins through the power of the Holy Spirit through the authority of the Church, and reminds us that we are good and radically loved.

Breaking the seal of the confessional is a serious crime and can result in automatic excommunication. While priests are certainly men, within the Sacrament of Reconciliation they are acting *in persona Christi*. Confidence in this standard allows me to bear my heart to Jesus Himself through His minister, the priest. In my experience, for those who long for the tangibleness of Jesus, this may be the closest we come to experiencing Him in the flesh. Of course Jesus is truly present in the Eucharist and I do not diminish that truth at all. Yet, in our humanness sometimes we simply need someone to look us in the eye and tell us that we are good, despite our weaknesses.

To conclude the discussion about when to speak the truth, the Church teaches us that professional secrets must be kept out of respect for the dignity of individuals or the common good. I recently attended an awards ceremony and was struck by the repeated comment, "we are so thankful for the service, effort, and contributions this particular person or group achieved. However, we cannot tell you any details of the projects for the safety of our nation."

Sometimes we cannot and do not need to know everything. Prudence is paramount and confirms to me the absolute necessity of the Church's guiding principles for all of human dignity and protection. Interference by the media in the private lives of public figures is to be condemned if it infringes on their privacy. With the advent of social media and technology we have more access to information than ever before. The *Catechism* reminds us in paragraph 2494 that "information provided by the media is at the service of the common good." Therefore we must use discernment and be compelled to practice moderation and discipline in our approach to mass media. We need to develop enlightened and correct consciences to resist unwholesome influences as well as avoid being led astray.

Truth, Beauty, and Sacred Art

The final section discusses truth, beauty, and sacred art. CCC 2513 summarizes this section where it states:

> **2513** The fine arts, but above all sacred art, "of their nature are directed toward expressing in some way the infinite beauty of God in works made by human hands. Their dedication to the increase of God's praise and of his glory is more complete, the more exclusively they are devoted to turning men's minds devoutly toward God" (*SC* 122).

Beauty conveys the truth of God. We are drawn to truth and beauty. "Sacred art is true and beautiful when its form corresponds to its particular vocation: evoking and glorifying, the faith and adoration, the transcendent mystery of God" (CCC 2502). When humans create art, we are co-creators with God. We utilize the talents and gifts He's given us to use to glorify Him. Bishops are called to keep and encourage beautiful art and remove inappropriate art from our Churches and Sacred spaces.

I was blessed to be able to be present when the artist who created mosaics for our church installed them. Mosaics are very intricate work and have a detailed installation process. As I watched her lovingly prepare each section of mosaic to be affixed to the wall, the light of Christ illuminated her face as she witnessed her time, effort, and skill come to life in our church through her art. What a gift!

Reflection Questions

Take some time to reflect upon the questions below. Consider writing in your Reconciliation journal or notebook of your choice. Invite the Lord to be present with you as you consider these questions.

- *What thoughts or feelings surfaced when reading this chapter?*
- *Did anything stand out to you as new or different than you had previously considered?*
- *Did the Lord convict your heart in a particular way?*
- *Are you moved to repent?*
- *Did you receive any interior movement in your heart, a consolation, or a deeper love for God or neighbor?*
- *What do you want to ask the Lord for now?*

Examination of Conscience—Eighth Commandment

Now that we have explored the Eighth Commandment, perhaps in greater detail than you have before, I invite you to sit with the Lord and review the following questions. What is the Lord saying to you? Holy Spirit Come!

1. *Have I lied?*
2. *Have I knowingly and willfully deceived someone?*
3. *Have I guarded against duplicity, dissimulation, and hypocrisy?*
4. *Have I failed to speak out in defense of the Catholic Faith, the Church, or of another person?*
5. *Have I perjured myself under oath?*
6. *Have I gossiped?*
7. *Have I committed detraction—by destroying or damaging a person's reputation by telling others about his faults for no good reason?*
8. *Have I committed slander or calumny—by making remarks contrary to the truth to harm someone's reputation or given occasion for false judgments concerning them?*
9. *Have I committed libel—betraying another's confidence through speech, deed, or in writing?*
10. *Have I been guilty of rash judgment?*
11. *Have I failed to make reparation for a lie I told, or for harm done to a person's reputation?*
12. *Am I guilty of flattery, adulation, or complaisance to encourage or confirm another in malicious acts and perverse conduct?*
13. *Am I guilty of boasting, bragging, or using irony aimed at disparaging someone?*
14. *Have I shared professional secrets?*
15. *Do I use social communication in moderation and discipline?*
16. *Do I respect and promote sacred art and remove that which is not in conformity with the truth of faith and authentic beauty?*

CHAPTER NINE

The Ninth Commandment—You Shall Not Covet Your Neighbor's Wife

No sooner had I placed my fingers on the keyboard to begin my workday, when my middle school son barged into the office. With urgency in his voice he said, "Mom, I have a question. Does the Ninth Commandment to not covet mean like their shoes, or their cars, or is it girls too?" A smile broke out over my face with his preciousness as well as the gift the Lord gave me to write this chapter! I tried to cover the basics in the five minutes we had before leaving the house. His eyes were as large as saucers when he declared, "oh my, all of my friends have committed adultery!" I laughed a hearty laugh and told him this topic requires more than five minutes before dashing off to school. We'd talk about it more in depth when we can give it its due time.

What does covetousness mean? CCC 2514 and 2515 offer an eloquent definition. Those paragraphs also direct us to an important Scripture verse. "Do not love the world or the things of the world. If anyone loves the world, the love of the Father is not in him. For all that is in the world, sensual lust, enticement for the eyes, and a pretentious life, is not from the Father but is from the world. Yet the world and its enticement are passing away. But whoever does the will of God remains forever" (1 John 2:15-17).

This Scripture passage communicates two important concepts. We must understand our primary purpose and goal in this life—heaven. We are transitory people. This world is not our primary home. We are pilgrims on a journey from this temporary world to the eternal world. From the beginning of time God has provided and continues to supply everything we need to make this journey. We do not have to grasp, hoard, and covet. We have to guard ourselves from the enticements of this world that threaten to distract us from our primary purpose and goal.

Once we understand we are made for the eternal world and not this transitory world, we can more clearly see how these worldly things distract us. These distractions often come when we shift our focus from contentment to comparison. When we begin to look around and compare our life to others, we have veered onto a dangerous road.

Many people unknowingly set themselves up with the desire to achieve all the worldly successes: wealth, fame, and power. Particularly regarding the Ninth Commandment, some people enter into marriage with an errant view of their spouse as someone to complete them or fill and heal all the ways they are lacking. This mindset is a recipe for disaster.

A friend shared her real and honest struggle in this area. The first years of her marriage brimmed with excitement and bliss. She and her husband both had jobs that fulfilled them and utilized their unique skills. They cared for and proudly showed off all their children's adventurous activities.

Then the daily grind began to set in. The stress of work, household management, and the uncontrollable nature of kids left her wiped out. She recounts that her husband used to compliment her, surprise her with flowers randomly, and overall be very attuned to her. He always knew what to say or do to help her feel fulfilled and valued. Over time, she felt this was no longer the case. He became grumpy, stressed, and isolated.

She watched with envy when her friends' husbands did for their wives what she wanted from her husband. She recalls that her heart was divided, resulting in bitterness, disobedience, and frustration. Nothing seemed good enough anymore. She realized how far she had strayed from both her husband and God.

This is what coveting does—it separates us from experiencing God's goodness, and it hinders our love for both Him and our neighbor.

This Ninth Commandment gets to the heart of the tension between the "flesh" and the "spirit." This is truly where we have to lean into the power of the Holy Spirit. These two final Commandments are where someone's efforts, resolve, and viability are put to the test. These two Commandments expose our hearts.

The more we are obedient to God and follow His commands, the more like Him we become and the easier (although never easy) it becomes to tame the lust of the flesh as St. John calls it. The next two paragraphs in the *Catechism* are rich with truth and beauty. They help to understand the significance of concupiscence upon our choices and our lives.

2517 The heart is the seat of moral personality: "Out of the heart come evil thoughts, murder, adultery, fornication. . . . " The struggle against carnal covetousness entails purifying the heart and practicing temperance:

Remain simple and innocent, and you will be like little children who do not know the evil that destroys man's life.

> **2518** The sixth beatitude proclaims, "Blessed are the pure in heart, for they shall see God." "Pure in heart" refers to those who have attuned their intellects and wills to the demands of God's holiness, chiefly in three areas: charity; chastity or sexual rectitude; love of truth and orthodoxy of faith. There is a connection between purity of heart, of body, and of faith:
>
> The faithful must believe the articles of the Creed "so that by believing they may obey God, by obeying may live well, by living well may purify their hearts, and with pure hearts may understand what they believe."

The more we allow our hearts to be purified by the fire of God's love, the more we are protected with a spirit of contentment instead of comparison.

While I know I don't go a day without sinning in some way, I have experienced the joy from striving to be pure of heart. We are so blessed in our Catholic faith to have such a motherly teacher in the Church. She shows us the way and gives us the blueprint or the instructional manual. The Holy Spirit, when invited in, gives us the power to live His way. In the times that we fall, and we will, we are given the balm of forgiveness through the Sacrament of Reconciliation. Honestly, what more can we ask for? We have been given a loving Father, Mother, Savior, and Spirit to lead us to the fullness of life. We must grab their hands with trusting confidence and proceed one step in front of the other. We are called to do our part. The battle for purity is real and fierce, but attainable with a docile and humble heart.

The Church doesn't leave us to our own devices. CCC 2520 outlines for us the tools we have access to and need to regularly use and sharpen:

2520 Baptism confers on its recipient the grace of purification from all sins. But the baptized must continue to struggle against concupiscence of the flesh and disordered desires. With God's grace he will prevail

- by the *virtue* and *gift of chastity*, for chastity lets us love with upright and undivided heart;

- by *purity of intention* which consists in seeking the true end of man: with simplicity of vision, the baptized person seeks to find and to fulfill God's will in everything;

- by *purity of vision*, external and internal; by discipline of feelings and imagination; by refusing all complicity in impure thoughts that incline us to turn aside from the path of God's Commandments: "Appearance arouses yearning in fools";

- by *prayer:*
'I thought that continence arose from one's own powers, which I did not recognize in myself. I was foolish enough not to know . . . that no one can be continent unless you grant it. For you would surely have granted it if my inner groaning had reached your ears and I with firm faith had cast my cares on you.'

With three teenagers left in the house, I am very grateful for the last paragraphs in the *Catechism* on this Commandment. The wisdom in the way modesty is communicated is so effective. Internal freedom comes through discipline. This is the incredible fruit of modesty.

Modesty protects the intimate center of the person. Modesty protects the mystery of persons and their love. Modesty encourages patience and moderation in loving relationships. We all want to be seen and loved, not used.

One of my rules for Sanchez Summer Nights is modest swimwear. This is not a prudish requirement hoping to dash my girls' hopes to wear a cute swimsuit. It's to communicate a message of their sacredness. It is a message that they are whole, complete persons who deserve the respect and dignity of their minds and souls as well as their bodies. It also communicates respect to the young men that we have solidarity with God's design for them to be attracted to beauty. It is a loving gesture to communicate that we also care about their mind, body, and soul and will do our part to help them in their mission of temperance and purity of heart. It is a declaration that we are called to love one another fully and filially. Our hearts are well-ordered when I can look at someone and see the individual as a person and not reduce them to lust. The final paragraph in this section is a very appropriate way to conclude.

> **2527** "The Good News of Christ continually renews the life and culture of fallen man; it combats and removes the error and evil which flow from the ever-present attraction of sin. It never ceases to purify and elevate the morality of peoples. It takes the spiritual qualities and endowments of every age and nation, and with supernatural riches it causes them to blossom, as it were, from within; it fortifies, completes, and restores them in Christ."

Reflection Questions

Take some time to reflect upon the questions below. Consider writing in your Reconciliation journal or notebook of your choice. Invite the Lord to be present with you as you consider these questions.

- *What thoughts or feelings surfaced when reading this chapter?*
- *Did anything stand out to you as new or different than you had previously considered?*
- *Did the Lord convict your heart in a particular way?*
- *Are you moved to repent in any way?*
- *Did you receive any interior movement in your heart, a consolation, or a deeper love for God or neighbor?*
- *What do you want to ask the Lord for now?*

Examination of Conscience—Ninth Commandment

Now that we have explored the Ninth Commandment, perhaps in greater detail than you have before, I invite you to sit with the Lord and review the following questions. What is the Lord saying to you? Holy Spirit Come!

1. *Have I been pure in heart and body?*
2. *Have I been modest in my dress?*
3. *Have I been modest in my actions? (avoiding media, advertisements, fashions, and prevailing ideologies contrary to modesty)*
4. *Have I been morally permissive?*

CHAPTER TEN

The Tenth Commandment—You Shall Not Covet Your Neighbor's Goods

The Lord is always concerned about our hearts; the center of our beings. This Tenth Commandment brings together many aspects of each of the preceding Commandments and challenges us to take a deep look into our hearts. It enjoins us to spend time focused on the motivations behind our actions and in all situations to be our barometer of holiness. CCC 2534 summarizes the Tenth Commandment.

God created all things good. We have natural desires, and this Commandment serves to remind us to keep desires rightly ordered. It cautions us against allowing our desires to exceed the limits of reason and prevent our drives to covet unjustly what is not ours. CCC 2536 clearly states:

> **2536** The Tenth Commandment forbids greed and the desire to amass earthly goods without limit. It forbids avarice arising from a passion for riches and their attendant power. It also forbids the desire to commit injustice by harming our neighbor in his temporal goods:
>
> When the Law says, "You shall not covet," these words mean that we should banish our desires for whatever does not belong to us. Our thirst for another's goods is immense, infinite, never quenched. Thus it is written: "He who loves money never has money enough."

It goes on to require that envy be banished from the human heart because envy can lead to the worst of sins. Wisdom 2:24 aptly reminds us "But by the envy of the devil, death entered the world, and they who are allied with him experience it." This is a sage and stern warning instructing us to guard our hearts against this dangerous sin.

Envy is a capital sin. It refers to the sadness at the sight of another's goods and the immoderate desire to acquire them for oneself, even unjustly. Envy can creep into our hearts like a silent dark stealth bomb.

St. Augustine saw envy as "the diabolical sin." From envy are born hatred, detraction, calumny (making false and defamatory statements about someone to destroy their reputation), joy caused by the misfortune of a neighbor, and displeasure caused by his prosperity.

Most of us have experienced envy to some degree or another. I remember when I was the lead facilitator for our mothers' group at Church. I watched in envy as some of the moms gracefully mastered the art of bringing their kids to daily Mass. These women seemed to have it all together with perfectly quiet and still children snuggled up next to them. Meanwhile my heart filled with embarrassment and shame with every wriggle, squawk, or innocent antic my children made. I instinctually gave them the "mom look." We all know that look! I found myself saddened that I didn't have what these other mothers seemed to have.

Thankfully the Lord was gracious with me and reminded me of several things. While the Mass is certainly the source and summit of our Catholic faith, He didn't ask me to go to daily Mass in this season of life. Daily Mass is a great good, but sometimes we can get distracted by doing good things even when they aren't necessarily what God asks us to do. The Lord helped me to uncover the motive in my heart. He helped me realize that even in this objectively great good, I performed my will and not His. He instead wanted me to love my children well and not make His house one to fear, dread, or be a source of draining joy.

Even to this day I invite my children to accompany me to daily Mass. Sometimes they come, sometimes they don't. But when they do join me, they experience a mother who delights in their presence right alongside the Father who delights in all of our presence. My joy is complete when my teenagers grab my hand and place it on their shoulder at Mass. They desire that connection and love that fills the atmosphere when we worship. It is as if my rubbing their shoulders, gently scratching their back, or playing with their hair, is the tangible presence of God's love reaching down to them. It is always an occasion to glance into each other's eyes, smile an insider's smile, acknowledging the love that flows between us. What a gift!

CCC 2544 issues a bold invitation:

> **2544** Jesus enjoins his disciples to prefer him to everything and everyone, and bids them "renounce all that [they have]" for his sake and that of the Gospel. Shortly before his passion he gave them the example of the poor widow of Jerusalem who, out of her poverty, gave all that she had to live on. The precept of detachment from riches is obligatory for entrance into the Kingdom of heaven.

This brings me into one of my favorite Scriptures that began this book. Matthew 6:33, states, "But seek first the kingdom [of God] and his righteousness, and all these things will be given you besides."

When we truly submit our entire selves to God Almighty, powerful, exciting adventures begin to open up around us. We are co-participants in the greatest story ever told! All of these promises of God found in the Ten Commandments are to ultimately lead us to see God face to face. Will it be a struggle? Absolutely! But as Hunter S. Thompson said in his book, *The Proud Highway: Saga of a Desperate Southern Gentleman*, "Life should not be a journey to the grave with the intention of arriving safely in a pretty and well preserved body, but rather to skid in broadside in a cloud of smoke, thoroughly used up, totally worn out, and loudly proclaiming,' Wow! What a Ride!'"[35] When we take this sentiment with Heaven as our targeted goal and purpose it truly is such a ride!

CCC 2548 and 2549 state:

> **2548** Desire for true happiness frees man from his immoderate attachment to the goods of this world so that he can find his fulfillment in the vision and beatitude of God. "The promise [of seeing God] surpasses all beatitude. . . . In Scripture, to see is to possess. . . . Whoever sees God has obtained all the goods of which he can conceive."
>
> **2549** It remains for the holy people to struggle, with grace from on high, to obtain the good things God promises. In order to possess and contemplate God, Christ's faithful mortify their cravings and, with the grace of God, prevail over the seductions of pleasure and power.

Oh blessed day when our hope is realized and we get to run into the arms of our loving Father who has been carrying us on this beautiful journey, surrounded by a cloud of witnesses exuberantly cheering us on and assisting us in ways we will come to know one day.

---

35 Thompson, Hunter S. (1997). *The Proud Highway: Saga of a Desperate Southern Gentleman (Fear and Loathing Letters)*. Villard.

We will conclude the Tenth Commandment with the final *Catechism* reference and more famous and exciting words from St. Augustine:

> **2550** On this way of perfection, the Spirit and the Bride call whoever hears to perfect communion with God:
>
> There will true glory be, where no one will be praised by mistake or flattery; true honor will not be refused to the worthy, nor granted to the unworthy; likewise, no one unworthy will pretend to be worthy, where only those who are worthy will be admitted. There true peace will reign, where no one will experience opposition either from self or others. God himself will be virtue's reward; he gives virtue and has promised to give himself as the best and greatest reward that could exist. . . . "I shall be their God and they will be my people. . . . " This is also the meaning of the Apostle's words: "So that God may be all in all." God himself will be the goal of our desires; we shall contemplate him without end, love him without surfeit, praise him without weariness. This gift, this state, this act, like eternal life itself, will assuredly be common to all.

Reflection Questions

Take some time to reflect upon the questions below. Consider writing in your Reconciliation journal or notebook of your choice. Invite the Lord to be present with you as you consider these questions.

- *What thoughts or feelings surfaced when reading this chapter?*
- *Did anything stand out to you as new or different than you had previously considered?*
- *Did the Lord convict your heart in a particular way?*
- *Are you moved to repent?*
- *Did you receive any interior movement in your heart, a consolation, or a deeper love for God or neighbor?*
- *What do you want to ask the Lord for now?*

Examination of Conscience—Tenth Commandment

Now that we have explored the Tenth Commandment, perhaps in greater detail than you have before, I invite you to sit with the Lord and review the following questions. What is the Lord saying to you? Holy Spirit Come!

1. *Have I envied others' possessions?*
2. *Have I been consumed by avarice? (Extreme greed for wealth or material gain)*
3. *Do I have a healthy detachment from riches?*
4. *Have I been seduced by pleasure or power?*
5. *Have I made choices out of greed instead of generosity?*

Sending Forth

Bringing us back to the opening analogy, my prayer is that you have felt the exhilaration of the initial assent of the roller coaster, the thrill of the wind of the Holy Spirit whipping through your hair and on your skin, and the unexpected excitement regarding a new conviction of faith during our time together. I pray that our journey challenged you, provided new insights, and allowed you to be wrapped in God's incredible love for you.

You are His beloved son or daughter created with a specific mission in mind. God has blessed you with special gifts and the grace for everything He invites you to pursue. You are a powerful warrior for the Kingdom. Lean into the Lord. Give Him your full heart and your complete yes. Allow yourself to be a miracle worker on His behalf. Speak and live the truth. Bear your crosses with humility and grace as a light for all the world to see. He loves you dearly and so do I!

Each one of us comes to a place in our lives where we squarely sit at a crossroad regarding our faith journey. It doesn't necessarily correspond with age, although there certainly can be a natural inclination to that correlation. At some point I was faced with making a whole-hearted decision.

Do I truly believe all this religious stuff or have my experiences and knowledge inclined me to reject these teachings? Was there enough evidence both academically and experientially for me to fully commit one way or another?

Each one of us has been willed into this world by Our Creator. Each one of us has been made in His likeness and image. Each one of us has been given the gift of free will with a capacity to give and receive the love we have been offered.

The Lord has offered us the Ten Commandments to guide and protect us. It might be helpful to think of sin as a choice between God's will and ours. You have diligently and perhaps painstakingly at times, read through the Church's teaching about God's will for us in our lives. Because of original sin, we certainly are inclined to choose our will over the Father's. Yet as Fulton Sheen so aptly noted, "It is not the wrong things one has already done that keep one from God; it is present persistence in that wrong."[36]

So how do we avoid present persistence in the wrong? Knowing what sin is and choosing to battle against it. The virtue of temperance can be of great assistance. Beg God for the grace of a pure heart, chastity, purity of intention, purity of vision, and perseverance through temptations and trials.

Additionally, fasting is a practice that puts our bodies in discipline with our mind. When we regularly deny our basic urges, in a healthy and temperate way, we can begin to train our eyes, ears, and bodies to listen and obey our will.

One word of caution: before beginning any practice of asceticism, always pray and ask the Holy Spirit for guidance and assistance. Sometimes we can get so zealous that we actually lose track of why we are fasting or performing other acts of mortification. The ultimate goal of every undertaking is a deep intimate relationship with God and to become holy as we ought.

The Litany of Humility is a powerhouse prayer. It concludes with one of my favorite reminders, *"that others may become holier than I, provided that I may become as holy as I should, Jesus grant me the*

36 Archbishop Fulton Sheen, *Peace of Soul*. Liguori, 1996. Page 185.

grace to desire it."[37] The evil one likes to attack every good work we attempt. If you find yourself comparing yourself to another's holiness, take a deep breath and start again in prayer. The Lord made each of us unique, and gave us gifts as St. Paul reminds us in Romans 12:3, "each according to the measure of faith that God has apportioned."

We aren't supposed to look at each other and desire to be the same. We are all to look straight into the eyes of Jesus on the Cross and ask Him to help us become exactly who we were created to be. Jesus achieved the greatest act of power on the Cross. He has offered us Himself wholly to redeem us. Don't leave this most amazing gift unwrapped.

St. Augustine offers us so much wisdom that still applies centuries later. In his book, *The Confessions of St. Augustine*, he states, "For my sin was that I sought out pleasures, grandeurs, and truths not in him but in his creatures, in myself and in others, and thus fell headlong into sorrows, confusion, and errors."[38] We sometimes hold onto our sins and those sins hold onto us. I sometimes joke that my extra baby weight must really love me because it holds onto my midsection with a death grip! On our own, we experience some degree of powerlessness to the enslavement of sin. But in, with, and through Jesus we have freedom.

We live in a time of access to many temptations that become a cause of struggle for us. That includes everything from constant advertisements to look a certain way, marketing messages to indulge in every whim, and images that, if not explicit, at least lead you down that path.

More than ever it takes supernatural help through the power of the Holy Spirit and surrounding ourselves with a strong community to help us stay accountable and on the right and true course. Gone are the days of parenting our kids without an eagle eye. The landscape has changed so much that it requires us as parents to adapt to the

---

37 https://www.ewtn.com/catholicism/devotions/litany-of-humility-245

38 St. Augustine, Fr. Gregory Pine O.P. (Author), Fr. Jacob Bertrand Janczyk O.P. (Author), Matthew K. Minerd (Editor). *The Confessions of St. Augustine*. (2023). Ascension.

changing landscape. No longer can we hope that our kids will make good choices because they are naturally good. There is so much temptation and lies lived out in the open, that we must bring our "A game." I hope this book is one means to prepare and arm you with the truth so you can boldly walk forward in faith and determination.

We have a perpetual invitation to humbly allow ourselves to sit at the feet of Jesus and learn from Him. We all have a good heavenly Father who stretches out His hand to us in desire to enfold us tightly in His strong, sturdy embrace of mercy, grace, and love.

More than any earthly father who teaches his son to throw a baseball, or his daughter how to dance, our Heavenly Father has given us His Word, His heart, and His very self—body, blood, soul, and divinity that we may become and experience all that He expressly created us for. Our question to answer is "Will we set aside any and everything that prevents us from accepting His free grace and gift to allow ourselves to be transformed by His love?"

God, through His Church, has also provided us with the Sacrament of Reconciliation to heal us. I have been amazed to witness what the Lord has done by means of this Sacrament over the past few years in my life. As my relationship with God has changed, so has my relationship with this incredible Sacrament.

For much of my young life, I immaturely viewed Reconciliation as a "time-out." It was a place where I had to gather my checklist of wrongdoings and account for them—not so much because I wanted to change, but more out of fear of the consequences if I didn't repent.

As I slowly matured in my faith, I went into Confession with a list of sins, feeling contrite in them, and for all intents and purposes made a good confession. However I encountered a problem. I also worked at the church. My confessor was someone I had to see and work with every day. Even though I appreciated the healing grace of the Sacrament, I sensed the Lord wanted to heal me more fully.

I noticed that I became uneasy in preparation to receive the Sacrament. Through God's grace I realized two extra sins were plaguing me: pride and vanity. Vanity showed itself though my wondering how this priest might view me. Pride also presented itself in my indignation that I kept repeating the same sins. Why couldn't I conquer them?

Romans 8:28 reminds us, "We know that all things work for good for those who love God, who are called according to his purpose." God took my pride and vanity and used it as a true source of healing.

I realized that I would never be without concupiscence for my sins—that is simply the human condition that I had to humbly accept. I had to take the next natural step. I asked God, "Lord, why do I continue to struggle with this particular sin? Please show me my source of woundedness in my heart that goes to that sin for comfort." The really awesome gift in praying this way, is that God always delights to answer these prayers. He constantly draws us near to Him, He pursues our hearts, He wants to heal those areas of brokenness and sin, and shine a light on those places of darkness.

St. John Chrysostom spoke words that resonate in my heart.

> Even if you do not confess, God is not ignorant of the deed, since He knew it before it was committed. Why then do you not speak of it? Does the transgression become heavier by the confession? No, it becomes lighter and less troublesome. And this is why He wants you to confess: not that you should be punished, but that you should be forgiven; not that He may learn your sin—how could that be, since He has seen it?—but that you may learn what favor He bestows. He wishes you to learn the greatness of His grace, so that you may praise Him perfectly, that you may be slower to sin, that you may be quicker to virtue. And if you do not confess the greatness of the need, you will not understand the enormous magnitude of His grace.[39]

A daily examen is vital to our spiritual growth. We must have the courage to ask the Lord and take accountability for our choices. There

39 Aquilina, Mike. *A Year with Church Fathers: Patristic Wisdom for Daily Living*. 2010 St. Benedict Press / TAN Books

are several formal examen prayers found online. Oftentimes mine simply looks like this:

Lord, be with me now. Help me to see as you see, as I honestly look over my day. I then review the events of the day and ask the questions: in what ways did I sin, and in what ways did someone sin against me? Come Holy Spirit and convict our hearts. Shine a light into our darkness.

I used to think, "how on earth can someone like St. Pope John Paul II go to confession every day?" Well, now I get it. As you get closer and closer to Jesus in your relationship and holiness, even the smallest of sins can seem both disgusting and disturbing to your soul.

There are many graces poured out in the Sacrament of Reconciliation. When we actively seek forgiveness and absolution we are provided the armor to battle. We come empowered to fight the good fight to truly slay those disordered desires—the desires of the flesh—from our hearts. It's important to note that the crushing of these desires is not an end to itself but rather it is what allows us to more perfectly mirror the image of God.

St. Paul declares so boldly in 2 Corinthians 3:16-18 "but whenever a person turns to the Lord the veil is removed. Now the Lord is the Spirit, and where the Spirit of the Lord is, there is freedom. All of us, gazing with unveiled faces on the glory of the Lord, are being transformed into the same image from glory to glory, as from the Lord who is the Spirit." Lord, let it be done unto me! Let my life shine your glory wherever I go! The Franciscan spirituality promotes a process of continual conversion. While we will never achieve perfection of holiness here on earth, I do believe our determined desire to ask the Holy Spirit to use His power to help us overcome sin and darkness is a request He simply cannot resist and He rejoices with us!

Thank you for journeying with me on this adventure of love. As we are concluding our time together here and continuing the adventure in our daily lives, will you join me in praying the prayer to the Holy Spirit? May God bless us all abundantly!

Come, Holy Spirit, fill the hearts of your faithful
and kindle in them the fire of your love.

Send forth your Spirit and they shall be created,
and you shall renew the face of the earth.

Let us pray.

O God, who have taught the hearts of the faithful
by the light of the Holy Spirit,
grant that in the same Spirit we may be truly wise
and ever rejoice in his consolation.
Through Christ our Lord. Amen.[40]

40 https://www.usccb.org/prayers/prayer-holy-spirit

Acknowledgments

What a gift to attempt to acknowledge so many friends who helped breathe life into this book. I thank God for His abundant grace to inspire and sustain this work. Thank you to my husband, Ricky, and our beautiful children, Kira, Myra, Caleb, and Christopher who give me the greatest honor of living out my vocation as wife and mother. Thank you to my parents and family who helped form me. I am also grateful for the intercession of the Cloud of Witnesses, including my mom and daughter, Gabriella. Thank you to those friends and family members who have given me permission to include parts of their sacred stories into this work.

During this project I sensed the Lord's invitation to pursue this endeavor in complete spiritual and material poverty. That in itself was a stretching and transformational work in my heart. I am blessed by my church community of innumerable prayer warriors who lifted me up throughout this project. I also want to thank everyone who generously offered their financial support. Thank you to my special friends who willingly offered their time and feedback along the way. Thank you Katelin for offering your editorial knowledge and wisdom. Thank you Rosemary for your creative design talents and expertise. Thank you Fr. Tom, Fr. Zack, Fr. Daniel, Fr. Jonathan, Fr. John Mark, Fr. Jason, Fr. David, Fr. Jim, Fr. Mike, Dcn. Richard, and Dcn. Rick for offering your theological insights and prayers. What a gift this project has been! Thank you Lord for inspiring this work and thank you readers for allowing the Lord to touch your heart through the reading of this book.

—With my love, Carrie

About the Author

Carrie Sanchez is a wife, mother of four, singer, author, and speaker—all which flow from her primary identity as a beloved daughter of God. She graduated *Cum Laude* with a BBA in Marketing from Texas A&M University. She has three Catechetical certificates from St. Junipero Serra Institute and will complete her Spiritual Direction certification from Divine Mercy University in 2026. She also contributed a chapter to the book *Cloud of Witnesses*. In addition to her primary vocation as wife and mom, Carrie spends her time offering financial coaching, volunteering in parish ministry, writing, speaking, and providing spiritual direction. She loves the Lord and sharing His message of hope and saving power!

Conversations with Carrie

Let's talk! Enter into a conversation with me. I cherish your comments, questions, and considerations. Use the QR code to be directed to a form where you can share your thoughts and insights with me.

Made in the USA
Coppell, TX
23 February 2026

72626563R00115